A ROADMAP TO REAWAKEN HINDUS
REBUILDING SANATAN
REVIVING TRADITIONS

Foreword by
Anand Ranganathan,
Author and Scientist

RISHABH KARNAWAT

BLUEROSE PUBLISHERS
India | U.K.

Copyright © Rishabh Karnawat 2023

All rights reserved by author. No part of this publication may be reproduced, stored in a retrieval system or transmitted in any form or by any means, electronic, mechanical, photocopying, recording or otherwise, without the prior permission of the author. Although every precaution has been taken to verify the accuracy of the information contained herein, the publisher assumes no responsibility for any errors or omissions. No liability is assumed for damages that may result from the use of information contained within.

BlueRose Publishers takes no responsibility for any damages, losses, or liabilities that may arise from the use or misuse of the information, products, or services provided in this publication.

For permissions requests or inquiries regarding this publication, please contact:

BLUEROSE PUBLISHERS
www.BlueRoseONE.com
info@bluerosepublishers.com
+91 8882 898 898
+4407342408967

ISBN: 978-93-5989-912-1

Cover design: Muskan Sachdeva
Typesetting: Rohit

First Edition: November 2023

Dedication

Extremely thankful to my brother who has been a constant pillar of support all along this wonderful journey.

Author introduction.

Dear Readers,

It is with immense joy and a profound sense of purpose that I present to you my debut non-fiction work. As an author, my journey has been a testament to an unyielding commitment – a commitment to revive Hinduism in its purest and most authentic form. My life's purpose has been, and continues to be, dedicated to aiding the youth and adults of this generation in their journey of self-discovery and cultural reawakening through an understanding of the true history and essence of Hinduism.

This book is a culmination of a lifelong mission to help Hindus reconnect with their roots, rekindle the cultural flame that has burned for millennia, and rediscover the profound wisdom that lies within the heart of Hinduism. It serves as a testament to the belief that the path to a brighter future is paved with a deep understanding of one's heritage.

Within these pages, you will find not just an author but a passionate advocate for the revival of a timeless culture. My goal is to unveil the rich tapestry of Hinduism's true essence, to shed light on its incredible history, and to ignite a fervor for cultural revival among my fellow Hindus.

As you embark on this literary journey, I invite you to join me in rediscovering the magnificent tapestry of Hinduism, a journey that has the potential to be transformative, enriching, and enlightening. This book is a humble offering in my quest to empower you with the knowledge, wisdom, and inspiration needed to revive our culture completely.

Thank you for choosing to be a part of this mission. Together, we can work towards a brighter and more culturally enriched future.

With gratitude and a sense of purpose,

Rishabh Karnawat.

Foreword

'REBUILDING SANATAN' is a must-read book for every Hindu to understand the true importance for reawakening of themselves before it is too late. The book should be read by all age groups including adults, but should be most importantly read by the youth.

Since Bharat got its independence, Hindus have been constantly discriminated against. Even after independence Hindu children were purposely and forcefully raised in such a way that they face a problem of inferiority complex whenever they say "I am Hindu". In this book Rishabh very rightfully and mindfully explains that how the blunder of making Hindus hate their own culture and look down upon it was started by the invaders. From talking about the MARXIST PHYCOLOGICAL WARFARE of which Bharatiyas became brutal victims to guiding the youth of this generation to take pride in being a Hindu, this book is a complete roadmap to reawaken every single Hindu.

The book tries to teach the readers about the true unsung heroes of this country who laid their lives for freedom. Rishabh also exposes the true reality of highly eulogized leaders with facts. It teaches one the importance of knowing the real history of Bharat and understand the importance of countless sacrifices which were made by our ancestors so that Sanatan Dharma survives. Most importantly, Rishabh very rightfully debunks the Aryan invasion theory which has divided Bharatiyas more than anything else along with several other such blunders which are still repeatedly caused even today by political parties to keep the Hindus divided for their personal benefit. This book not only awakens the Hindus but motivates them to be united by knowing and understanding the right knowledge.

Rishabh very carefully exposes the real faults in the education system of Bharat which has failed to nurture a profound appreciation for

Hindu culture and wisdom over a very long period of time and has led to such circumstances, But the book also describes a few sets of values which people need to follow on their individual capacity to make sure that Hindus are again awakened, reawakened and united.

Lastly, 'REBUILDING SANATAN' is not just a book. it is a transformative voyage into the heart of Hindu culture and identity. It invites readers to harmonize the ancient wisdom of Sanatan Dharma with the demands of the modern world, fostering a renewed sense of connection and pride in being Hindu. This book is a testament to the enduring vibrancy of Hinduism and the incredible potential of those who seek to safeguard and share its timeless wisdom.

~ ANAND RANGANATHAN, AUTHOR AND SCIENTIST.

Nirvana Shatakam also known as Atma Shatakam is a six-level compilation of verses recited by Sri Adi Shankaracharya. Sri Adi Shankaracharya had composed several hymns on Bhagwan Shiva and other Gods and Goddesses. It was believed that He Himself was the manifestation of Bhagwan Shiva.

Nirvana Shatakam is based on the concept of Advaitha (non-dualism). It means that Jeevathma (Personal soul) and Paramathma (Divine soul) are not two different aspects but one and the same. The aim of Jeevathma shall be to attain the level of Paramathma. This is the manifestation of self-realization.

Sri Adi Shankaracharya had travelled the entire length and breadth of Bharath (Hindustan) seeking and spreading the knowledge.

As believed, Sri Adi Sankara as a young boy of eight years was strolling in the neighborhood of the banks of river Narmada.

Sri Sankara was in search of a spiritual teacher (Guru) for himself. He met Seer Sri Govinda Bhagavat Pada. On spotting Sri Sankara, the seer simply asked "Who Are You?".

It is believed that Sri Adi Shankara had recited the six stanzas known as 'Nirvana Shatakam' or 'Atma Shatakam'. After listening to these recitations, the Seer had accepted Sri Adi Sankara as his disciple.

Nirvana Shatakam is composed on the principles of Oneness, i.e, the transformation of inner soul (Jeevathma) into Bhagwan Shiva (Paramathma) through self-realization.

This attainment of supreme soul is possible only through self-liberation, that is letting go of material attachments. "Vana" means the support structure such as wood or cloth and "Nirvana" means unleashing of all the attachments.[1]

1.

मनो बुद्ध्यहंकार चित्तानि नाहम्
न च श्रोत्र जिह्वे न च घ्राण नेत्रे
न च व्योम भूमिर् न तेजॊ न वायुः
चिदानन्द रूपः शिवॊहम् शिवॊहम् (1)

mano budhDh-yahankaara chiththaani naaham

---

[1] https://www.hindugallery.com/nirvana-shatakam/

na cha Shrothra jihvae na cha GhraaNa naethrae

na cha vyoama Bhoomir na thejoa na vaayuh

chidha-anandha roopah shivoaham shivoaham

Meaning - My mind is not tied up with the intellect, concept on inner self and the reflections of individualism. I am liberated from my mind. I do not possess the smelling and hearing senses. I am beyond all the five senses. I am neither the sky, nor the earth (combines water and land), nor the fire and nor the wind. I am beyond the five elements. I am certainly the blissful and eternally happy Shiva, the supreme consciousness.[2]

2.

न च प्राण संज्ञो न वै पञ्चवायुः

न वा सप्तधातुर् न वा पञ्चकोशः

न वाक्पाणि पादौ न चोपस्थपायू

चिदानन्द रूपः शिवोहम् शिवोहम् (2)

---

[2] https://www.hindugallery.com/nirvana-shatakam/

na cha praaNa sanjnoa na vai panchcha-vaayuh

na vaa saptha-Dhathur na vaa panchcha-koashah

na vaakpaaNi paadhau na choapa-sThapaayoo

chidha-anandha roopah shivoaham shivoaham

Meaning - I am not the breathing life (existence) and I am not the five types of breath {Pancha Prana means five types of breath such as Prana, Apana, Samana, Udana and Vyana}. I am not the seven dhatus, i.e the elements in the body which help in sustenance. {Sapta Dhatu means seven elements in the body such as rasa or lasikaa (nutrient fluid in water form), rakta (blood), maaṁsa (muscle and tissue), meda or vasaa (fat tissue), asthi (bone tissues, tendons and ligaments), majjaa (bone marrow) and shukra (generative tissues)}. I am not the five wraps around the soul. {Pancha kosha / five wraps denote annamaya kosha [Physique], pranamaya kosha [Energy], manamaya kosha [Mind], vignayamaya kosha [Wisdom] and anandamaya kosha [Eternal Bliss]}. I am not the tools of existence such as hands or feet or voice or other appendages. I am certainly the blissful and eternally happy Shiva, the supreme consciousness.

3.

न मे द्वेष रागौ न मे लोभ मोहौ

मदो नैव मे नैव मात्सर्य भाव:

न धर्मो न चार्थो न कामो ना मोक्ष:

चिदानन्द रूप: शिवोऽहम् शिवोऽहम् (3)

na mae dhvaeSha raagau na mae loaBha moahau

madhoa naiva mae naiva maathsarya Bhavah

na Dharmoa na chaarThoa na kaamoa na moakShah

chidha-anandha roopah shivoaham shivoaham

Meaning - I have no abhorrence or revulsion; Have no fondness or affection;

I have no greed or pride or hallucination or arrogance or jealousy or any such feeling.

I have no obligation or duty, no wealth, no desire and no end.

I am certainly the blissful and eternally happy Shiva, the supreme consciousness.

4.

न पुण्यं न पापं न सौख्यं न दुःखम्

न मन्त्रो न तीर्थं न वेदाः न यज्ञाः

अहं भोजनं नैव भोज्यं न भोक्ता

चिदानन्द रूपः शिवोऽहम् शिवोऽहम् (4)

na puNyaM na paapaM na saukhyaM na dhhukham

na manthroa na theerThaM na vedhaah na yajnaah

ahaM BhoajanaM naiva BhoajyaM na Bhokthaa

chidha-anandha roopah shivoaham shivoaham

Meaning - I am not the holiness or the viciousness; I am neither comfortable nor sorrowful.

I do not need mantras; I am not ascetic; I do not need holy scriptures; I do not need havan (homam).

I am neither the food nor the eater who enjoys the food.

I am certainly the blissful and eternally happy Shiva, the supreme consciousness.

5.

न मृत्युर् न शंका न मे जातिभेद:
पिता नैव मे नैव माता न जन्म
न बन्धुर् न मित्रं गुरुर्नैव शिष्य:
चिदानन्द रूप: शिवोऽहम् शिवोऽहम् (5)

na mruthyur na shankaa na mae jaathi-bhedhah

pithaa naiva mae naiva maatha na janma

na bandDhur na mithraM gururnaiva shiShyah

chidha-anandha roopah shivoaham shivoaham

Meaning - I have no fear on death as I do not have death; I have not parted from my inner soul, no qualm on my subsistence; I have no bias on caste basis.

I do not have a father; not have a mother; not have a birth.

I am not a relative; not a friend; not a teacher; not a disciple.

I am certainly the blissful and eternally happy Shiva, the supreme consciousness.

6.

अहं निर्विकल्पो निराकार रूपो
विभुत्वाच्च सर्वत्र सर्वेन्द्रियाणाम्
न चा संगतं नैव मुक्तिर् न मेय:
चिदानन्द रूप: शिवोऽहम् शिवोऽहम् (6)

ahaM nirvikalpoa niraakaara roopoa

viBhuth-vaachcha sarvathra sarvaendhri-yaaNaam

na chaa sangathaM naiva mukthir na meayah

chidha-anandha roopah shivoaham shivoaham

Meaning - I have neither attributes nor differences; I am liberated and I have no form;

As I am supreme; I have no wishes for my organs as I am everything;

I have no attachment; I have no salvation; I am always redeemed.

I am certainly the blissful and eternally happy Shiva, the supreme consciousness.

Nirvana Shatakam shows the light on the toughest question on earth, i.e. "Who am I?". It examines the soul, the mind, the virtues, the vices, the relationships, companionship, the body organs, the wishes, the needs and all the material attachments and concludes that all such inner and outer accessories are just appendages and that only the Athma (Soul) does matter and the rest of the things are immaterial.

Nirvana Shatakam unifies the Athma (Soul) with God by eliminating / nullifying all the worldly attachments both internal and external. This unification with God liberates the soul through self-realization and makes us to understand that our Athma (soul) is commensurate with the entire universe[3].

Hare Krishna Hare Krishna, Krishna Krishna Hare Hare

Hare Rama Hare Rama, Rama Rama Hare Hare.

---

[3] https://www.hindugallery.com/nirvana-shatakam/

Prologue

With no experience of writing a book but a vast experience of preaching knowledge about the Sanatan dharma and telling people its true importance I am writing this book to inform everyone about a roadmap which I have designed by myself to reawaken, rebuild and revive the Sanatan Dharma. I have designed this book in such a way that the following roadmap talks about history of Hindus from hundreds of years to what is happening in the present day. In this book I have proven how Hindus have been actively brainwashed and forced to forget their own rich culture. I talk about how the society in our own country Bharat has been gradually designed in such a way that we start forgetting our own culture and start looking down upon it. This book which is filled with harsh but true facts easily makes you understand how Hindus have been tortured and murdered since hundreds of years. From dividing Hindus to trying to establish a discriminative rule over them, this book covers most of the important facts about the atrocities Hindus have faced over years. But the book does not stop only on mentioning facts and harsh truths, but this book will guide every individual on how to contribute for the rebuilding and reawakening of our dharma. It talks about the reasons why the discriminations against Hindus are reaching a tipping point, and what Hindus have to do to stop it. We as proud Hindus have to realise the importance of reestablishing our cultural roots or we will be the ultimate preys of the genocidal killings. It is my request that every person reads this book till the end and invokes a sense of responsibility to save our culture. Reading this book will give you the answers to many questions you must be having inside you, also this book guide on how efficiently you can contribute to protect our culture. It is a high time now that Hindus get discriminated again and again. From talking about M.K Gandhi who is referred as so-called Mahatma, who says "Hindus should not harbour anger in their hearts against Muslims even if the latter wanted to destroy them. Even if the Muslims want to kill us all we should face death bravely. If they established their rule after killing Hindus, we would be ushering in a new world by sacrificing our lives." To Jawaharlal Nehru, who became the so called first prime minister of the independent Bharat who was nothing but a cheap British slave constantly trying to impress the Britishers and discriminate Hindus. I also talk about the unsung heroes because of whom the independence was truly possible and who had a major role in securing Hinduism. These great personalities include Narayan Apte, Subash Chandra Bose, Swatantra Veer Savarkar, the legendary Nathuram Godse and many more. This book will surely invoke a sense cultural belonging towards our own motherland which is Bharat. The following 6 chapters will be your transformation from a normal Bhartiya citizen to a responsible Hindu Bhartiya citizen.

Contents

Author introduction. ....*iv*
Foreword ....*vi*
Prologue ....*xviii*
Be united 1
Know the real history. 27
Forgotten legacies. 47
Never forget the atrocities 62
We were never a defeated civilisation. 101
Please read scriptures. 112
Epilogue *117*

Be united

ब्राह्मणक्षत्रियविशां शूद्राणां च परन्तप |
कर्माणि प्रविभक्तानि स्वभावप्रभवैर्गुणै: || 41||

brāhmaṇa-kshatriya-viśhāṁ śhūdrāṇāṁ cha parantapa

karmāṇi pravibhaktāni svabhāva-prabhavair guṇaiḥ[4]

Translation - The duties of the Brahmins, Kshatriyas, Vaishyas, and Shudras—are distributed according to their qualities, in accordance with their guṇas (and not by birth).[5]

Many of you reading this book will be already knowing the above-mentioned verse and its meaning. For those who don't know let me

---

[4] https://www.holy-bhagavad-gita.org/chapter/18/verse/41
[5] https://www.holy-bhagavad-gita.org/chapter/18/verse/41

elaborate it in a very basic and fundamental way. Since the beginning of our childhood, we have been taught in schools about how the Varna system worked in Ancient Bharat and we were always told our society was tremendously discriminative towards particular castes. But is it really true? Or is it part of the anti-Hindu narrative which was formed a few decades ago in pre independent Bharat and is still carried forward shamelessly. Let us understand how Hindus were brainwashed to fight against each other.

The most obvious rather most important question is if there is not a single Hindu scripture which talks about dividing Hindus in castes on the bases of their birth, how people started following this practice. How did people make these caste systems so rigid in society? And why such people became so discriminative in nature. The answer is very simple. We were FOOLED. To understand it in a much more precise way let me elaborate the true meaning of the four Varnas. These were not divided on the bases of work a particular community followed, rather they were divided on the Karma of people. This means it is very specifically said that it depended on how a man lead his life. If His/her karma were very spiritual, pure divine then he or she was a brahman, but if his/her karma were not good, completely in the mode of ignorance and there was no divinity present then of course such a man would be called a Shudra. With this basic knowledge you should understand how the caste systems were actually divided which were based upon the way of life and mode of goodness a particular person had. It had nothing to do with birth. So how did this original concept of Varna change into this rigorous form which made us Hindus divide so much over the decades? All this started on the arrival of Christian missionaries in our country, followed by the Britishers, Gandhi and much more. (Note- I don't take past all the way back to Mughals because I think analysing and fixing the mistakes of the recent past is much more important, but I will surely mention the atrocities done over Hindus and Mughals in upcoming chapters.) First the missionaries began the brainwashing on a very minute level but who knew this would transform in such a big blunder today.

The very famous and wicked Missionary we all know about is St. Francis Xavier. We were all taught about this man in school where they brazenly only mentioned him as a missionary and never told how evil work he did against Hindus on their own land. Let me quote some lines by this man before I elaborate further. "The Brahmins are the most perverse people in the world…. They never tell the truth, but think of nothing but how to tell subtle lies and to receive the simple and ignorant people… [6]They are as perverse and wicked a set as can anywhere be found, and to whom applies the Psalm, which says: 'From an unholy race, and wicked and crafty men, deliver me, Lord'. The poor people do exactly what the Brahmins tell them…. If there were no Brahmins in the area, all Hindus would accept conversion to our faith'."[7] And this is the very beginning of the great blunder which continued and continued and is still continuing. Let me mention another quote from this evil man about Hindu idols. These references will give you idea how wicked

---

[6] https://www.hindujagruti.org/hindu-issues/hatkatro-khaamb/francis-xavier
[7] https://www.hindujagruti.org/hindu-issues/hatkatro-khaamb/francis-xavier

these people were and how evil their intentions were." I DO NOT KNOW HOW TO DESCRIBE IN WORDS THE JOY THAT I FEEL BEFORE THE SPECTACLE OF PULLING DOWN AND DESTROYING THE IDOLS BY THE VERY PEOPLE WHO FORMERLY WORSHIPPED THEM"[8]. Such people started preaching wrong knowledge to people and started intense indoctrination. The reason behind is simple, they knew the only way to rule over Hindus and gradually convince them to convert is divide them and brainwash them. Brahmins who were the most intelligent class of that time were the one's responsible for educating people and preaching them knowledge about their culture. The missionaries very cleverly knew that the only way to divide the Hindus is to break the backbone of the source of their knowledge. And this backbone were the brahmans. The missionaries started to fill up brains of local people, making them hate the brahmins and go against them. This was the best weapon they could use. Once people go against the

---

[8] https://www.hindujagruti.org/hindu-issues/hatkatro-khaamb/francis-xavier

brahmins, the source of righteous knowledge of people comes to an end. And from here the further brainwashing starts. In order to promote conversions and create an atmosphere of mental terror, St. Francis Xavier and his missionaries saw to it that the Hindus were tortured by all possible means, particularly where the evidence against the accused (foisted cases for Inquisition and Conversion through fraud, force and inducement!) was incomplete, defective or conflicting. there were specially designed sharp instruments with spikes for cutting the ears of Hindus, for breaking their legs and shin, for disembowelling them over the rack, for breaking their jaws, for tearing their tongues and finally there was a specially designed Christian equipment (designed with Christian compassion of rigorous mercy!) for tearing apart the female breasts. Very unfortunately thousands of Hindus who were tortured and killed by St. Francis Xavier and his missionaries have not left behind contemporary records relating to their sufferings, trials and tribulations.

All this gradually led to a sense of misunderstanding amongst various individuals and they started doubting the brahmans of that age. Their children were taught a very different perspective about the brahmans and the hate started to grow gradually in the hearts of people against each other and specially in the hearts of other castes against brahmins. All this was very carefully and cleverly carry forwarded by various missionaries, and the division of Hindus was started. After the idea of conversions and so-called Brahmanical superiority had sparked amongst the individuals, the British arrived in Bharat. So now you know, whenever people question Hindus on the so-called caste discrimination which they think we have, just answer them with all above mentioned points I have mentioned and this will be enough for them to realise the original essence of Sanatan Dharma. And those who still after so much references and evidences still don't believe in this untold history, just understand they have been blinded by mode of ignorance.

One of the most important things which we need to follow for staying united and unanimous is we need to stop considering ourselves a very elite and superior class. The moment we start showing someone within our own community superiority and Elite Ness, we play a role of stupidity on our behalf. This behaviour of showing superiority will rather weaken the unity. In this Kaliyuga majority of humans are same. All of them have a mode of ignorance inside them, even if it is less or more. The more we show this kind of behaviour which is filled with ego to people who we think are less superior compared to us, we start dividing ourselves over and over. So always remember treat everyone with kindness and that's what is been taught us in our scriptures. To save our dharma and protect it the very first step is to keep our ego aside, and this is what It actually means to keep our ego aside. This short story will help you understand that the go you carry or anyone you know who carries ego is nothing but a foolish creature. When Mahmud of Ghazni came to India for the first time to attack on us and plunder the wealth. He had to fight a war with a king known as Jaypaldev. Unfortunately, because these barbaric warriors of Ghazni did not even follow the rules of a war, Jaypaldev was defeated. Later he was treated by humiliation by Ghazni after which he was set free to go on a condition that Jaypaldev pays a sum of a specific amount to Ghazni (In those days Bharat was richer than any other civilisation on planet. It was richer than your wildest imagination.) Jaypaldev on returning to his kingdom gave up all his ornaments and swords and wore Sanyasi white cloth. He said in a public announcement that "I have failed in my duty of protecting you, hence my dharma on this Bhumi is finished. I handover this kingdom to my capable son and henceforth he has the responsibility of protecting you." After saying this in a huge public announcement, Jaypaldev lied down on a bed of woods and set himself on fire.[9] Such incredible legacies are what we carry forward. Such great individuals have set their foot on this Pawan Bhumi. So, next time you show ego to someone over superiority, always remember it is all the darkness of ignorance. People have no idea how foolish they are when they show their stupid eliteness.

Now allow me to give you a little more insight on how this "Divide Hindus" propaganda has

---

[9] https://youtube.com/shorts/tLLfIUOBtzI?feature=shared

continued for years and is still continuing. In your school life or collage life or probably in the later part of your life you must have had come across that how Gandhi tried to eliminate the caste system. Another big blunder which you should know about. Gandhi to glorify himself tried to become famous in all sections of the society. Instead of trying to bridge the gap between the different sections of the society by using the divine Vedic knowledge and wisdom he started to indirectly glorify the rigorous caste system more. This man called the weaker sections "Harijans". Already mentioning this is my personal opinion on the acts he did which were technically not supposed to be done. Instead of calling weaker sections with these terms, he should had told them and also the other sections of the society the truth about how thus caste system was followed in Bharat, but this man was so miserably drowned in the desire of being the only leader of the people in the pre-independent Bharat, he started this blunder. More often than not these things psychologically divide people more. And this particular opinion of mine comes from a very brilliant person I met. Unfortunately, the person was blind but when I asked him the question "sir what do you think should be actually done to bridge the gap between the normal and especially abled people". he gave me a very beautiful answer, he said "The society should completely stop all kinds of discrimination, may it be good or bad. When the people will even stop labelling us as people with super powers or people with 6 senses, we will be continued to be discriminated. "I found this answer so meaningful and precise. It was so relatable to this condition. The more you start finding ways to add differences, the discrimination doesn't stop, rather it increases. Gandhi should had for once kept his desire aside of becoming the hero in people's heart and should had done something more sensible like preaching the right knowledge to the people. This would better abolish the caste division then and there itself. But unfortunately, a few more series of incidents continued and abolishing it remained a dream.

Even till this day if we look closely this has not stopped at all. The so called Indian National congress tries to divide Hindus on the basis of the caste system just for vote bank politics. Rahul Gandhi, who is the most prominent leader of the congress party says lines in press conference like " jitni abadi utna hak"[10] and tries to provoke discrimination more on the grounds of caste system. He says a caste census should be done and population of OBC (other backward classes) , SC(scheduled castes), ST(scheduled tribes) should be thoroughly divided. What is the need for divide when all the OBCs, STs and SCs are Hindus. We all are equal. This kind of propaganda spreads more hate amongst the people and Hindus start dividing more. This wrongdoing does not stop here. The media channels do the most immoral work. They bring castes in every crime telecasted. When a heinous crime is done on a particular person who belongs to the so called OBC background, they will never mention the person to be a Hindu but they will always mention a person belonging to the OBC caste. This is not case with the Muslims. When a Muslim man is found to be a victim of crime,

---

[10] https://timesofindia.indiatimes.com/india/why-rahuls-jitni-abadi-slogan-against-spirit-of-constitution/articleshow/100216352.cms?from=mdr

Be united

he is not mentioned as a Muslim belonging to the minority community of Muslims. To be clear Muslims have 7 different types within themselves. Slowly and gradually but rather at a very good pace this starts brain washing people. So now always remember, these people will always try to divide you on the basis of caste. We don't have to fall in the trap of such evil wicked people. We are UNITED HINUDS. We are equal. We have to be together. We have to fight this battle of community divide together. So always keep in mind, nobody can break us when we stand UNITED.

The biggest hoax which I will reveal now is the 'Aryan invasion theory'. This particular theory which was invented by those colonialists has caused tremendous damage to our culture, country and community. Whatever the terms we use which are called "Adivasis or Mulnivasis". All these names and terms were used by colonialist. It was not us who coined these terms, these terms were coined by them to create this another blunder. Probably know other wrong knowledge has caused so much damaged to Bharat, the way this theory has caused. From here on I will provide references and evidences to clearly prove that why this 'Aryan invasion theory" was a hoax and what was the main reason behind inventing such a fake theory. The reason is very SIMPLE, Divide the Hindus against themselves. You will soon understand how dangerously this theory divided the Hindus of Bharat. Let me debunk this dogma of ARYAN INVASION THEORY for you.

For those who don't really know what Aryan invasion theory (AIT), here is a short description about what it actually is and how was it imposed by those evil colonialists upon us. The Aryan invasion theory dates back to the period when there was colonial rule in India. Max Muller, is known to be the one who first proposed the theory of Aryan invasion. If I have to say point wise, the key features of this theory included the following things. And remember, it is the bedrock upon which the Indian history is written.

India's original inhabitants were "dark-skinned" Dravidians, who built a peaceful, highly developed, near-utopian urban civilization in western India and present-day

Pakistan: the so-called Harappan or Indus valley civilization.

India was invaded and conquered from the West by nomadic people called the Indo-Aryans around 1500 BCE. These Indo-Aryans were of European origin (hence white-skinned), and spoke Vedic Sanskrit. They destroyed the indigenous Dravidian civilization, subjugated the natives, and forced them to migrate to India's South.

The Indo-Aryans then composed the Vedas, and imposed Hinduism and the caste system upon the hapless Dravidians and other indigenous peoples of India.

So basically, this theory meant that our culture Hinduism doesn't have his roots in Indian sub-continent, rather Hinduism is written by people who came here all the way from Europe. And the way crooked Winston Churchill said "Indians missed the bus of civilisation". This man didn't even know how technologically advanced the Indus valley civilisation was. But coming back to the debunking of this theory, let me tell you point by point why this theory is completely fake and a hoax.

1. The science of genetics has revolutionized the study of ancient history and given researchers an unprecedented ability to uncover the details of humanity's past. India has lagged behind in genetic research, and the government of India has in the past prohibited foreign researchers from collecting genetic samples of Indians. This restriction has been removed of late, and, as a consequence, a new picture of Indian history is emerging.

Consider the following:

a. This research paper demonstrates the absence of any significant outside genetic influence in India for the past 10,000 – 15,000 years.

b. This research paper excludes any significant patrilineal gene flow from East Europe to Asia, including India, at least since the mid-Holocene period (7,000 to 5,000 years ago).

c. This research paper rejects the possibility of an Aryan invasion/migration and concludes that Indian populations are genetically unique and harbour the second highest genetic diversity after Africans.

d. These three research papers demolish the AIT. They conclusively and irrefutably prove that there was no Aryan invasion circa 1500 BCE.

2. The supposed Aryan-Dravidian divide <u>is a myth</u>. <u>The Nature report</u>, which cites three genetic studies, demonstrates that most Indians are genetically alike, belying the hypothesis of an Aryan-Dravidian dichotomy. <u>Other studies</u> have also demonstrated that people in north India are no different from those in the south and that all share the same genetic lineage. The R1a1a haplogroup is found in high frequencies in north Indians as well as south Indians, in tribal communities, and in 'low castes' as well as in 'high castes. Claims that the Dravidians belong to a separate, non-Hindu civilization are also discredited by ancient Tamil Sangam literature, which dates back to c. 300 BCE. The Mahabharata is mentioned in the oldest Tamil Sangam literature. The Vedas and the Ramayana are also mentioned in Sangam literature.

Sangam literature mentions the whole of India, starting from lands to "the north of the Himalayas", which contradicts the claim that the Dravidians were confined to the south of India. The above evidence, taken together, demonstrates the genetic and cultural continuity of India from the north to the south, and proves that the artificial concepts of the "Aryan-Dravidian divide" and the 'high caste'- 'low caste' divide have no basis in fact.

3. The Sarasvati is extensively mentioned in the Rig Veda, India's foundational literary text. It is referred to as "greatest of rivers", "glorious", "loudly roaring", and "mother of floods". This clearly refers to a mighty river in its prime, not one in decline. This falsifies the AIT account that the Rig Veda was composed after a purported Aryan invasion/migration circa 1,500 BCE, and indicates that it was composed closer to 5,000 BCE when the river was last in its prime per the results of Sarkar et al's study. This raises serious questions about the AIT's validity. India's "mainstream" historians dismiss the Rig Veda as

mythology. This is a naive and subjective assumption that betrays an unscholarly bias on their part. If the Rig Veda is mythology, then so are <u>Herodotus'</u> fanciful and inaccurate <u>Histories</u>. Herodotus, however, continues to be cited as a reliable historian. These smacks of double standards. The Rig Veda is certainly less fanciful than Herodotus' Histories. Moreover, it is a veritable treasure that gives us the earliest literary insight into human society and thought. As such, it must be taken seriously.[11]

It is clear that there is layer upon layer of archaeological, literary, linguistic, and, most importantly, genetic evidence that forms a consistent, repeated, and predictable pattern that debunks the Aryan Invasion Theory and supports the Indigenous Aryans Theory. These layers of evidence, taken together, paint a vast canvas and prove that:

1. The Indo-Aryan people and languages originated in the Indian subcontinent.

---

[11] https://indiafacts.org/aryan-invasion-myth-21st-century-science-debunks-19th-century-indology/

2. The Vedic civilization and the Indus valley civilization (Sindhu-Sarasvati civilization) are one and the same.

3. The Rig Veda was composed closer to c. 5,000 BCE when the river Sarasvati was last in its prime, than to c. 1,500 BCE when it dried out. This makes the Rig Veda a strong candidate for being the world's oldest known literature.

4. Rather than being a religion of invaders, Hinduism is indigenous to India and has its origins in the very beginning of the Sindhu-Sarasvati civilization.

5. North Indians and South Indians are genetically and culturally alike. The Aryan-Dravidian divide is a myth; it has no basis in fact. The 'high caste'-'low caste' divide also has no basis in fact.

6. Indian civilization is a continuous, unbroken tradition that dates back to the very beginning of the Sindhu-Sarasvati civilization, at least 9,500 years before present. This makes India not only the world's oldest civilization, older than Mesopotamia and Egypt, but also the

world's oldest continuously existing civilization. This makes India the true Cradle of Civilization.

7. Indo-Aryans carrying R1a1a lineages expanded westward thousands of years ago, conquering and populating territories as far west as Europe. They were the most successful conquerors in human history. Their descendants are the Slavs (Russians, Ukrainians, Czechs, Poles, Slovaks, Serbs, Croats, Macedonians, etc.), the Scandinavians, and many others.

8. In other words, the new evidence comprehensively debunks the 19th century's colonial Aryan Invasion Theory and its late 20th century refinement, the Indo-Aryan Migration theory.[12]

Here are all the facts you need to completely debunk the Aryan invasion theory. This particular theory has caused miserable divide amongst Hindus. Later what happened was, when those nasty Britishers came up with this theory, they started imposing this on south

---

[12] https://indiafacts.org/aryan-invasion-myth-21st-century-science-debunks-19th-century-indology/

Indians to create divide. Fortunately, Kerala and Karnataka didn't fall for this trap but unfortunately Tamil Nadu did. Gradually all the people from that state started accepting this theory and started considering themselves as different from the Hindus living in that north, which was originally not the case. They accepted that they are the Dravidians and Hindus from north are the Aryans. This created a sense of divide and they started developing a feeling of separation. This is the reason today we see a very different behaviour of Tamilians on the topic of declaring Hindi a national language or may it be something else. Thereby British didn't only divide Hindus in caste system by theory but also divided Hindus on the basis of region they lived in. So probably the last question in your mind must be, where did these two words come from, 'Aryans' and 'Dravidians'. Here is your answer for that, This story dates back to the time of Adi Shankaracharya. In those days Buddhism flourished immensely. Hinduism was gradually declining. This is when Adi Shankaracharya took the responsibility of reviving Hinduism again. He did the most Bhartiya thing anyone can do, he didn't wage a war for conversion, rather he used 'Shastras' to win over people. This means he used the idea of debate to revive Hinduism again. He started debating with Buddhist scholars, and decided that, if Adi Shankaracharya wins, the scholar with whom he was debating would convert back to Hinduism, if the latter wins, Adi Shankaracharya would get converted. Nobody was able to defeat the great Adi Shankaracharya. Later he travelled from the southern region all the way till north. On this journey he finally reached the most prominent Buddhist scholar who was living in current Bihar, called Mandana Mishra. So, the big question came up, who would umpire the debate. So, after a discussion Adi Shankaracharya recommended Mandana Mishra to make his wife the umpire. Mandana Mishra's wife accepted to do that. The first question she asked was, "who are you?". Adi Shankaracharya said "Travid Shishu". Travid means where the 3 coasts meet. And Shishu means child. Therefore, he was referring that he is from the southern region of Bharat. Later the British pounced on the 'Travid' word which later became 'Dravid' due to mis-pronunciations. And talking about the word 'Aryan', there is no such word as Aryan in Hindu scriptures. The word Arya is mentioned, which means a civilised man.

And this is how the Hindus were immorally and wickedly divided.

Be united

ADI SHANKARACHARYA- THE GREAT SAINT RESPONSIBLE FOR REVIVING HINDUISM AGAIN IN BHARAT.[13]

---

[13] https://imgk.timesnownews.com/story/Shankaracharya_Jayanti.jpg

ADI SHANKARACHARYA REVIVING HINDUSIM AGAIN.

Know the real history.

How many of you actually apply a Tilak while going out of your house, or going to your offices, schools, colleges or any other place. Let me be very clear on this topic. Whenever we see a person who is working with us or studying with us applying tilak on his forehead, don't we get a feeling that this man is a right winger. Just observe the current society now, how the emotions and feelings of people have transformed gradually by labelling their own beliefs as extremist. And this is not only about tilak. There are a lot of things we see which people do, which are very clearly their own day to day beliefs but unfortunately all this societal change has transformed these beliefs into extremist, right winger and what not. This is the true reality of our society.

Let me throw some light on the foolish rules which schools make. I have experienced it myself, that school doesn't permit Tilak, they don't permit 'Kadha' which is a sacred bangle Hindus wear. I myself saw it in my school, that for students to wear that 'Kadha' they had to write letter for seeking special permissions. What type of society is this where we need to seek permission from people to practice are own customs and traditions, what type of society is this where Hindus are labelled as extremists and right winger when they apply Tilak on their forehead or follow any other tradition. And now when we see the current life of people, I know that the society has transformed in such a way that even if a mother applies a Tilak on her beloved son's forehead, the miserable environment of those schools will knowingly or unknowingly force him to wipe it off. This is the destructive grooming that has been happening. This needs to be changed drastically, and if this is not changed now, you will soon see a society where every child has forgotten his or her own culture. And this doesn't sound as serious as it actually is, this will result in mayhem. People will start believing in wrong things which we call WOKISM in today's modern world. Another harsh truth will be if Hindus stop taking pride in practicing their own culture, conversions will increase so rapidly and mark my words, conversion and wokism is only in control in India because there is a sizable amount of people who still take tremendous amount of pride in practising Hinduism. But when I see the younger generation, I don't really see a safe future until we take efforts to educate them properly. Here is an example which will give you a better understanding of how children are brainwashed, and if they don't get brainwashed, they get brutally beaten up. A 10th class student was allegedly beaten up by the principal of the school along with the class teacher for writing "jai shree ram" on board. He was beaten up so brutally that he had to be hospitalised. This is the current scenario. So, watch, observe and learn.

This is a very important thing I would like to address, when the whole Nupur Sharma incident happened about which I will talk briefly in upcoming chapters, Hindus were at pain to accept the fact that Shiva Linga is a

Linga. They started to defend themselves by calling Shiva Linga a form of energy and what not. Why can't you just accept the fact that a Shiva Linga is a Linga and it is a demonstration of Raudra or masculinity or potency. It is a demonstration of masculinity. Stop defending yourself when someone questions you about this, take pride in saying the truth. We are Hindus, the oldest living civilisation which was the most civilised society. We were just brainwashed by saying that we were barbaric, but it was not true. It was the other way around. If you want an example for how civilised we were, here is a piece of information you should know. A few years ago, when there were massive floods in the regions of Pakistan where the Indus valley civilisation resided, surprisingly the places which were excavated for research didn't get washed by floods, the only reason was the drainage and water flowing system of canals in the civilisation was so advanced that even after such massive floods, the region did not get washed, rather the canals which were made using cement by the engineers washed away within minutes after the floods arose.

Know the real history.

A very surprising incidents which we see in the current generation or current society is that when a particular public figure who is civilisationally and culturally a Hindu visits a temple or does something which his or her traditions tell him to do, people start calling it a propaganda, show-off and what not. Recently I came across a news with a picture of the legendary actor Rajni Kant toughing feet of Chief Minister Yogi Adityanath,[14] people started all the hate comments on social media apps saying Rajni Kant being elder to Yogi shouldn't had done that, but little do they know, this is the richness of our Hindu culture where we worship the divine monks and their sacrifice of the material life. So, all this when happens shapes the view point of the society and the view point does the brain washing of the people in that society. Ahead of this, this chapter will be a deep dive in knowing the true history of our culture, traditions and the bloodshed which happened due to the countless

---

[14] https://www.hindustantimes.com/entertainment/tamil-cinema/rajinikanth-reacts-after-touching-up-cm-yogi-adityanaths-feet-101692665201205.html#:~:text=Actor%20Rajinikanth%20reacted%20days%20after%20a%20section%20of,to%20touch%20the%20feet%20of%20Yogis%20or%20Sanyasis%27.

sacrifices of people to save Hinduism from the rule of Islam for 600 years and from the rule Christian colonialist for 200 years. I assure, whoever reads this journey of saving Hinduism even after the countless terror attack, he or she will be immensely proud to be a Hindu and practice this incredible culture.

Not taking back this story to Mughal reign, as many of you know how cruel and evil it was which wiped off almost 100 million innocent Hindus and millions of other Hindus were converted. I will begin this story with the time of colonial rule, widely known as the British rule. This story is about ideological subversion which happened. This subversion happened with various stages involved in it, and this subversion was done with full support of Nehru and Gandhi. The highest art of warfare is not to fight a war with weapons, but fighting a war with mind, THE PHYCOLOGICAL WARFARE. [15]The ideological subversion is a part of the Marxist system of phycological

---

15

https://r.search.yahoo.com/_ylt=Awrgwqv.UEll2i40zBBXNyo A;_ylu=Y29sbwNncTEEcG9zAzEEdnRpZAMEc2VjA3Ny/RV =2/RE=1699332478/RO=10/RU=https%3a%2f%2fprachyam.c om%2f/RK=2/RS=q6TIW3xOQQ7yUZ9PCjjiAZK1l4s-

warfare. Our Bharat was totally prosperous with rich knowledge, good manners, rich culture, fascinating traditions and most important of all great scholars like Rishi Munis. The ideological subversion is a process of to change the perception of reality to such an extent, that despite of an abundance of information nobody is able to come to sensible conclusions. It is a great brain washing process which goes very slow and is divided into four basic stages:

1. Demoralisation- Bharat was immensely connected with its own dharma, the closest English word for dharma can be religion, but dharma doesn't have any English translated word. So, for better understanding we will use the word religion. In case of ideological subversion via religion, destroy it and ridicule it. Replace it with various sects' cults and take it away with the supreme purpose of religion which is to keep people together. Therefore, British executed the first step by understanding the Hindu Dharma, which was yet most prominent even after 600 years of Islam rule. Megasthenes, writes in

his book Indica that Hindu Dharma is divided upon the way of life you live. It is most difficult to become a brahmin because a brahmins life is most difficult due to immense Bhakti and worship of lord. The book is written 2300 years ago. Thereby the concept of Brahminical patriarchy was started by British. The contribution of brahmins to this society is unmatched, it is because of them Hindus survived the Islamic terror. They knew brahmins were the brains of Hinduism, so they directly targeted the brain of it. Crooked Colonialist did the act of understanding the Hinduism but rather they wrote it in all wrong ways and by mass printing, started preaching wrong and fake knowledge. The very first man to be known to become a slave of Britishers is Ram Mohan Roy. This man was the first British agent who was Indian to start preaching wrong Hinduism to people. That's a different thing that he later converted to Christianity and was buried in London. Many such people like Ram Mohan Roy came because they were given bribe of Respect and a good life by

Britishers. Later Gurukuls were broken down, Brahmin teachers and Gurus were killed. Every source of right knowledge for Hindus was blocked. And as I mentioned earlier, people were immensely divided. 1835 was the year when William Bentick brought the English Education Act. Now gradually things started declining much more, students were trained by the colonialist to look down upon their own culture. Gurukuls were finished. [16]

2. Destabilisation- Dropouts and half-baked intellectuals were now taking positions in the power of government, civil services, businesses, mass media and education system. You are stuck with them now and you cannot even get rid of them. Now the brainwash was on such a level that even the authentic information was not able to teach people the right knowledge. Even if you prove white is white and black is black, they were programmed in such a way that they

---

[16]
https://r.search.yahoo.com/_ylt=Awrgwqv.UEll2i4OzBBXNyo
A;_ylu=Y29sbwNncTEEcG9zAzEEdnRpZAMEc2VjA3Ny/RV
=2/RE=1699332478/RO=10/RU=https%3a%2f%2fprachyam.c
om%2f/RK=2/RS=q6TIW3xOQQ7yUZ9PCjjiAZK1l4s-

would not believe. In this loop the Indians who worked for British received money, power and respect. The clever British knew that their rule on India would not stay forever, therefore a British man Allan Octavian Hume founded the congress party. Yes, you read that right, Congress party was founded by Hume and not Gandhi. So now the freedom fighters were also appointed by British, the reforms were done by British and also the country was totally run by British. The dream of Hindvi Swaraj was failing. Now the country was stuck in a loop. Now these Indian agents of British who are half-baked intellectuals, start holding a sense of political power in the country. One of the most prominent British agents was Motilal Nehru. Slavery of British was in the blood of Nehru family. Now the country was totally destabilised. Motilal became the king maker of the congress and, later declared his son Jawaharlal Nehru as congress President. And this marked the beginning of dynastic politics in congress which still goes on. And simultaneously Mohammed Ali Jinnah was

Know the real history.

being cultivated in England for future use. Now the root was Dravidianism is set, the root of Khalistan has been set and much more is done.[17]

3. Crisis- In this stage Gandhi made Nehru the congress President with his free will and non-democratically. In a bench of 15 leaders, 12 leaders voted for Sardar Vallabhai Patel. Not even one voted for Nehru. But both crooks, Gandhi and Nehru conspired this. In fact, Nehru did want to be the last English Man to rule India. Now at this stage population is sick and tired. And here comes a man known as so-called saviour, who Nehru pretended to be. Crisis started taking place at this time. Civil wars broke out. Many Hindu-Muslims clashes were occurred where thousands and thousands of Hindus were killed. America started a new foreign policy in 1947 to eradicate communalism. Other than listening to Big Daddy America, Britain had

---

[17]
https://r.search.yahoo.com/_ylt=Awrgwqv.UEll2i4OzBBXNyo A;_ylu=Y29sbwNncTEEcG9zAzEEdnRpZAMEc2VjA3Ny/RV =2/RE=1699332478/RO=10/RU=https%3a%2f%2fprachyam.c om%2f/RK=2/RS=q6TIW3xOQQ7yUZ9PCjjiAZK1l4s-

no choice but to leave India immediately. Partition was mapped out via the Project Balkan and rest is the history. Nehru first rejected this partition as he was scared of the bloodshed that would take place, but his dear friend Edwina Mountbatten handled him very well.[18]

4. Normalisation- Now the Partition was done and independence was achieved but with the will of British agent Gandhi, Nehru was made the first prime minister of independent India. Nehru was nothing less than an Anglo- Indian Marxist leader. And most importantly the colonialism which left India now returned again but with the name of modernity. In those days Baba Ramchandra, a very prominent leader said "what will be the difference if these people who were servants of British, rule India again". The white rulers will leave India but now India will be ruled by their back rulers. And this is what exactly happened. And

---

18

https://r.search.yahoo.com/_ylt=Awrgwqv.UEll2i4ozBBXNyo A;_ylu=Y29sbwNncTEEcG9zAzEEdnRpZAMEc2VjA3Ny/RV =2/RE=1699332478/RO=10/RU=https%3a%2f%2fprachyam.c om%2f/RK=2/RS=q6TIW3xOQQ7yUZ9PCjjiAZK1l4s-

now the normalisation was successfully done.[19]

In conclusion to all these a series of events occurred in the history, which shaped the life of Bharatiyas and especially shaped the life of Hindus. The congress leaders made a lot of secret agreements which are not yet been made public by the Britain Government, nor the Bharat Government. India's first governor general was Mountbatten, who was recently found to be a paedophile. The second governor general was Raj Gopala Charya, who not only made the plan for India's partition but was also supported by Winston Churchill.[20] That Churchill who mascaraed millions of Indians in a man-made famine in Bengal. Nehru brought out the concept of secularism which was later added by his daughter in the preamble of India. Even after been recommended by people that

---

[19] https://r.search.yahoo.com/_ylt=Awrgwqv.UEll2i40zBBXNyoA;_ylu=Y29sbwNncTEEcG9zAzEEdnRpZAMEc2VjA3Ny/RV=2/RE=1699332478/RO=10/RU=https%3a%2f%2fprachyam.com%2f/RK=2/RS=q6TIW3xOQQ7yUZ9PCjjiAZK1l4s-

[20] https://r.search.yahoo.com/_ylt=Awrgwqv.UEll2i40zBBXNyoA;_ylu=Y29sbwNncTEEcG9zAzEEdnRpZAMEc2VjA3Ny/RV=2/RE=1699332478/RO=10/RU=https%3a%2f%2fprachyam.com%2f/RK=2/RS=q6TIW3xOQQ7yUZ9PCjjiAZK1l4s-

the concept of secularism is baseless in Bharat, Nehru had to do it. The constitution was deliberately made in such a way that it appeases Muslims. A Hindu dharma-based constitution was more than enough to bring perfect law and order, but causing blunders is in blood of congress. Ambedkar did propose the idea of uniform civil code, but Nehru said "no". Nehru said "we cannot say Muslims to change, but we can definitely make the Hindus change." Nehru's secularism was simple, control over Madrasas was communal, but control over temples was secular. Reconstruction of Somnath temple was communal, naming roads on Mughal invaders as secular.

One of the biggest blunders done was appointing Maulana Azad as the first education minister of the independent Bharat. By this, such an education system was made which we all know how it grooms us. It makes children less patriotic. It makes them question the bravery of their own leaders of the past who sacrificed so much for the motherland.

The journey of setting the education system is also much more complicated than it seems.

Know the real history.

Indira Gandhi opened all doors for the education ministry to programme the education in such a way that Marxist would. This was all result of KGB (Komitet Gosudarstvennoy Bezopasnosti) agents infiltrated in India like Krishna Menon and many more. Indira Gandhi sold everything, the future of the country, children, youth and people, everything to the Soviets. Just because she was desperately greedy for the power. She wanted to become the prime minister. Various history writers and people went to USSR. But for them, they were just a bunch of political prostitutes and nothing else. All this shaped the way education system was made in Bharat.

The limits crossed when Indira Gandhi appointed Syed Nur Hassan as the education minister of India. This opened the doors to the worst phase of the Indian education system. Akbar who should be known to kill more than 30,000 peasants and countless Hindus, was labelled great in our history textbook. Much more lies were mentioned which will take at least 50 volumes of such book to debunk. It is so simple to understand that when you write your history textbooks in such ways where the

Muslim rulers are portrayed as villains and what they truly were, you can never ever do Islamization of the country. But the textbooks were written other way around, and the reality is in front of us. We can see how children are been groomed in our nation.

Now the final part of this chapter comes where we understand how the Idea of Nehru's modern India created a catastrophe for the Bharat and resulted in a phycological mayhem. Gradually due to such series of events, people literally started worshipping the foreigners. People started thinking the original modernity is not in following the traditions and culture, rather behaving like those foolish foreigners. I still remember my grandfather telling me, when he was a child, the foreigners when they came to India, people saw them in such a way as if they were a celebrity. They were treated like a current day actor or actress in those days. Now the bigger identity than being rich or poor was are you a foreigner. Schools started teaching, British gave us Railways, Mughals gave us architecture and Greeks science. Middle class started to assume that prosperity and modernity is acting and living a lifestyle like foreigners. People started to hate their own culture and dharma, is it necessary to hate your own culture to become modern? People who were beating the hell out of us Bharatiyas, today we aspire to become like them, we start to worship their lifestyle. Media channels, movies and drama. Everything was made in such a way the people start considering the English Men more superior.

One very destructive thing which happened was flourishing of English medium schools. Students who were supposed to be taught in their native language were now forcefully taught in English language, which is yet considered more superior. The bigger problem is more than 50 percent of the efficiency of the brain is used to decode the English language by the child. This results in decrease in efficiency of learning the cognitive skills by the child's brain. People were judged if they are literate or illiterate on the basis of how well they spoke English. The things we fought for so many decades again returned in a completely new form. And in this ecosystem globalisation added more petroleum in the burning fire. The pictures of cities like New

York were shown in such a way that students build a desire of going and learning there. The Hollywood movies which showed smart CIA agents playing with toy guns excited the youth and drove the Indian youth towards itself. And this was the journey of breaking Bharat so much that people now desire a life of those who ruled over them for so many decades. And this is the true history which you were supposed to be taught.

But now with this chapter coming to an end, the bigger question arises, who are the real heroes for us? Even after so many invasions and conspiracies, who helped in the survival of Sanatan Dharma? You just understand the fact, wherever Islam ruled, all the countries got 100 percent converted into a Muslim country. Today's Iran was earlier Persia where all the Zoroastrians and Parsis lived. Within 15-20 years all the Parsis and Zoroastrians were wiped out. Those who survived escaped to India. (Ratan TATA is a Parsi). Christianity converted so many countries. But even after 2 consecutive rules of Islam and Christianity respectively, Hindus managed to be the 80 percent population of the country. How was

Know the real history.

this possible? Well, all this happened because of those legendary unsung heroes about whom you should know and should had been taught in school but you were not. In the next chapter I will talk about those unsung heroes about whom you should know but you don't. These are the real heroes because of whom are great Sanatan Dharma still survives.

JAWAHARLAL NEHRU.

I DON'T THINK MUCH MORE DESCRIPTION IS NEEDED, BUT THIS IS HOW NEHRU WAS GUIDING BHARAT TOWARDS "MODERN INDIA".

Forgotten legacies.

"GARV SE KAHO HUM HINDU HAI"
BALASAHEB THACKERAY.

This chapter will disclose the true voices of valour. The following chapter will be a deep dive into understanding the true heroes of our nation. According to what I have understood over the past few years by researching about the education system of the country that, even if the whole country knows sub-consciously that the education systems is total garbage, it is not been changed drastically. The NCERT books or the CBSE curriculum is not being changed even after every Bharatiyas knowing, that the history which is being taught is extremely wrong and from a wrong perspective. And I have completely given up on any government in power to change the education system. So now the question arises that what is the other option or alternative to help children gain the right knowledge about our past. Well, in this midst of darkness the only light of hope I see is getting self-taught about the originally history from great historians and scholars like Vikram Sampath and Meenakshi Jain. And trying to preach the real knowledge to people on your individual capacity, especially to children and youth who have been brainwashed completely by Left-Liberals and secularist of our country. Try showing them videos of YouTube channel like Prachayam rather than allowing them to watch the leftist channel of Dhruv Rathee. Such youtubers like Dhruv Rathee who call themselves so-called fact-checkers, wrongly prove our history of Mahabharata and Ramayana FALSE and brainwash children. These people with their half-baked knowledge try to spread a wrong propaganda, so please preach the right knowledge on your individual capacity. Furthermore, I will try to talk about all those unsung heroes about whom you either don't know or you have a very wrong perspective about them. I sincerely apologise if I don't mention about any important freedom fighter in this book, this book is too short to mention about the countless sacrifices done by legends to save and carry forward Sanatan Dharma.

1. Nathuram Godse- I am very much sure that I am going to get a lot of backlashes by mentioning this man as a hero, but this book will be incomplete without mentioning the great sacrifices done by Nathuram Godse for Hindus and also for Bharat. A lot of the facts from this book have been taken from the testimony of the Nathuram Godse which was not allowed to publish by the congress government. The testimony was later written by Gopal Godse, who was brother of Nathuram Godse. Nathuram Godse was a man who belonged to RSS (Rashtriya Swayamsevak Sena) and an editor in a newspaper called Hindu Rashtra. Nathuram Godse never had any personal enmity against Gandhi. In fact, Nathuram Godse believed in non-violence more than Gandhi did, but later he was portrayed as a very violent Hindu nationalist, a terrorist and so much more. Gandhi believed in "Ahimsa Parmo

Dharma." But Godse believed in "Ahimsa Parmo Dharma, Dharma Himsa Tathyva Cha." Godse believed the that non-violence is the first priority in life, but he has better understanding of Hindu scriptures than Gandhi ever had, that's why he knew the meaning of second line also, it was Violence is needed when you need to protect your dharma, which is Sanatan Dharma. As I mentioned earlier Godse had no enmity with Gandhi, yet he killed him. Godse mentioned 148 different reasons to kill Gandhi in his testimony. And these reasons justified the crime he committed. Of course, I cannot mention all the reasons, but I will mention the very final reason which triggered Godse to assassinate Gandhi and save Bharat and the Hindus. After independence, India was supposed to pay 55 crores to Pakistan, but the Kashmir issue was not resolved. Therefore, Sardar Patel came up with a mind-blowing plan of telling those crooked Pakistanis that if the Kashmir issue is not resolved, 55 crores will not be paid. Gandhi opposed this idea and started a fast unto death, until Bharat pays

55 crores to Pakistan. This made Godse think, if such fasts keep happening, soon Bharat will be extremely damaged and so will the Hindus. Thereby he killed Gandhi even after knowing that with the end of Gandhi's life, he will end his own life as well. The book mentions so many more reasons, which can prove Gandhi to be one of the most anti- Hindu people. Reflect on this incident and just imagine how ill-treated were Hindus since the time of partition. Godse even after justifying his crime was sentenced to death. This was the wrong information programmed in your brain, that is the reason you do not appreciate the contribution of Godse in preventing the future blunders against Bharat and also against Hindus. And he is the first unsung hero to save Hindus and Bharat. I request each and every one of you to read the book "Why I killed Gandhi" written by Nathuram Godse, which was banned by the Congress Party, which was against the right of freedom of speech. Later, after Nathuram's brother was set

free, after his jail term, he published the book. It was Gopal Godse who published it.

2. Baji Rout- This is probably the first time you are hearing name of this boy. Yes, he was a boy who is known to be the youngest freedom fighter to gain martyrdom at the age 12. On the night of 11th October, when he refused two British police to give them a ferry across the Brahmani River, he was shot dead by them. This boy died at the age of 12 in a peaceful protest against the British police. These were the great lived and died for our nation and motherland. This is boy is not only a role model for me but should be for every child, youth and adult. Such legendary people have stepped on our motherland that is the only reason we are surviving today. He is the person we should be taught about. In today's modern world children try to be superior and make other people feel inferior. These are what children of this generation are busy in. And on the other side, we have people like Baji rout who gave their lives at the mere age of only 12 to help the motherland gain freedom. And the tragedy of the situation is

Know the real history.

we are not even taught the name of this boy in our history textbooks. So, this is what you should truly know about.

3. Swatantra Veer Savarkar- Here, this is a man who led Bharat's first organised secret society known as Abhinav Bharat. He was the first one to start burning the foreign clothes with couple of bunches of students. He was a scholar who was graduate from the Ferguson collage located in Pune. Later he went to London to study law, where he also wrote a book named the war of Indian Independence of 1857. This book became a perfect guideline for future revolutionaries. Later this book was also translated in many languages by Subhash Chandra Bose. Bhagat Singh even got the second edition of this book published. It was a roadmap for the future revolutionaries. Most importantly, he spent 12 long years in the most terrifying jail of Kalapani, where he was brutally tortured. Moreover, he also spent 2 years in the jail, in India. The women of Savarkar's house, were now on the streets, requesting for livelihood. Even the utensils of the house were auctioned and

sold. His degree was taken away from him, that's why Savarkar is always mentioned as metric pass which is completely wrong. Even after all this, when he was sent back from Kalapani, he was kept on a house arrest for several years in his own house in Ratnagiri. 27 years of his life was snuffed out. And today people sitting in air-conditioned rooms try to prove that he was a traitor and what not. These crooked people don't even know what really is freedom struggle, they just have to pass these nasty comments for useless publicity and a couple of votes. Kalapani was such a terrifying jail, it was said that it is better to die that to live in Kalapani. And this man spent 12 years of his life in Kalapani. A fact of the matter which you should know is that not a single congressman was sent to Kalapani, It was all revolutionaries who were sent there.[21]

4. Sardar Vallabhbhai Patel- As many of you may know about this legendary man who was famously called the Ironman of

---

[21] https://youtu.be/u0L0O_yssJ4?feature=shared

Know the real history.

independent Bharat. He was given this title because his contribution of uniting 565 princely states of Bharat together to form a single nation, which he did dinglehandedly was incredible. The man who was originally elected as the prime minister by a bench of 15 leaders, but was later sidelines by the Gandhi and the congress has done an incredible contribution towards our motherland Bharat. Just imagine, in this world of Mobile phone where you can do so much work at an ease of a click, you cannot even reunite the concept of Akhand Bharat. But this man without any technology of communications, cars and flights for traveling continuously. Travelled all across India and not only travelled but convinced 565 princely states to be united to form Bharat. This is the true achievement of this man who people fail to appreciate. I am thankful to the Modi government that recently this man was given the respect which he deserved by making the statue of unity. His contribution is unmatched and can be never be forgotten by Bharat. This man was the one who stood up for Hindus and requested for construction of the Somnath temple. He is the real heroes of Hindus.

This list would go on and continue endlessly until I don't write at least a fifty or more volumes to talk about every single unsung hero of this motherland. But these four people which I personally thought can inspire every single generation to love the motherland and our own Sanatan Dharma. The contribution of these people and more like them can never ever been forgotten. It is my humble request to each and every one of you to read about them and understand about their sacrifices as much as possible. This will again help our sub-conscious brain rebuild our Sanatan Dharma, and also reawaken every single Hindu in our civilisation. This makes me so sad that I couldn't write about every single sacrifice, but whatever I wrote about is to make you realise that you are living such a relaxed life is not because of the 2 or 3 people about whom you have been constantly taught about at every stage of life, but you are alive because of the endless and countless sacrifices of Hindu warriors and Hindu freedom fighters who gave up their life, family, everything for the future of this nation.

These things should make you understand that the way people are being brainwashed is unbelievable. We are not only taught history in such a way that we forget our culture but we are also taught to forget the lives which were lost for our own nation. Mind my words, the more we promote and propagate this kind of education system, the more we move towards our own end. And once we reach a point of no return, where not a single child doesn't care of his or her own cultural identity, the consequences are such that they cannot even be described in words.

As you may know now, about how some great unsung heroes, it is important to know about contributions of some people in the recent times who actually helped Bharat save and revive Hinduism. It has become an identity of an educated person in Bharat to call himself a secular or a liberal. People have been thinking that it makes the much more modern by saying 'I am a liberal' or 'I am a secular'. And we cannot even blame such people anymore, because of the last stage of the phycological warfare of the Marxists people, they have been completely brainwashed. These people are brainwashed in such a way that now it has become impossible to convince them or make them understand the importance of people like Bal Thackeray who courageously took stand for Hinduism. Some of the people even feel embarrassed to support such people in public such as offices and schools. I only have one thing to say to them, that is the day when they see a mob of some so-called peaceful community outside the house, that's when they will forget all this liberal and secular hoax and understand the true importance these Hindu leaders. Why do we take a backfoot when it comes to supporting people like T. Raja Singh of Hyderabad or Bal Thackeray of Maharashtra. This list does not only stop here, there are so many more Hindus who really need our support but nobody actually does support. If we do not support those Hindus who actually take stand for us then we will fail ourselves as a community. Our own government also fails in recognizing the contribution of such individuals. This is the reason we need to support these people who at least stand up in defence for our community. As I said earlier also that take pride in being a Hindu, exactly in the same way take pride in supporting the Hindus who stand for you. Only we can stop the atrocities which are happening against people of our community by taking a public stand for them and protecting them in all ways possible. Stop trying to be 'secular' and 'liberal' just to show how educated you are. It is not even the representation of how educated you are, rather it shows how mediocre and foolish you are. Support those people who come on roads and protest for you, because in the end it is only going to be them and nobody else who will come to save you when a mob reaches outside your house. And please don't be embarrassed of supporting them. I have myself seen people in many schools and offices who make anonymous social media accounts to post content about Hinduism and Hindu leaders who are yet fighting in either courts or on roads to protect our community and our rights. The day those people will stop making such anonymous accounts just because they are embarrassed to show how much the love their culture, that will be the day we all we light a spark of change in the mindset of people. So always remember, being secular and liberal is not the proof of how educated you are, it only proves that how foolish and mediocre you are.

Know the real history.

VEER SAVARKAR AND THE TERRIFYING KALA PANI CELLULAR JAIL WHERE HE WAS IMPRISONED.

Never forget the atrocities

"Sanatan Dharma is like Malaria, dengue and corona. It shouldn't be opposed rather it should be eliminated." Statement made by the spoiled brat of Tamil Nadu Udhaynidhi Stalin. [22]This is not it. Another leader from the same party as Udhaynidhi which is DMK says "Udhaynidhi was soft, Sanatan Dharma should be compared to HIV or leprosy", this was a statement by A. Raja. [23]The blunder does not stop here,

---

[22] https://www.indiatoday.in/india/story/udhayanidhi-stalin-dmk-tamil-nadu-sanatana-dharma-madras-high-court-criticism-2458809-2023-11-06
[23]
https://r.search.yahoo.com/_ylt=Awr49Ix2UkllTSczNwNXNyoA;_ylu=Y29sbwNncTEEcG9zAzEEdnRpZAMEc2VjA3Nj/RV=2/RE=1699332855/RO=10/RU=https%3a%2f%2fwww.news18.com%2fpolitics%2fdmks-a-raja-likens-sanatana-dharma-to-social-plights-like-hiv-leprosy-bjp-calls-it-hinduphobia-8567806.html%23%3a~%3atext%3dAmid%2520the%2520ongoing%2520controversy%2520over%2520it%252C%2520DMK%2520MP%2cof%2520Sanatana%2520Dharma%2520to%2520malaria%2520was%2520%25E2%2580%259Crelatively%2520mild.%25

congress president Mallikarjun Kharge's son Priyank Kharge also supports these nasty statements. In fact, the major truth which a lot of people do not know is that the conference where Udhaynidhi spoke these lines was titled, Sanatan Dharma eradication conference. What the hell is happening in this country? When a woman who just quoted some lines of the scriptures is boycotted officially or unofficially by the government but a spoiled brat who tries to provoke people openly to protest against a particular community is not even condemned immediately. Not a single so-called liberal or secular came in the picture to condemn this horrendous act by these ministers. All these seculars and liberals were hidden in their den. What type of secularism is this where a single community is constantly oppressed by a so-called secular. Why is it that every single time on Hindus are lectured over secularism even when they accept all religions in Bharat which is their holy land. Every single time it is Hindus who have to suffer. May it be the Ram Mandir case which took more than 30 long

---

E2%2580%259D/RK=2/RS=3pBlVaCEIslHNvVdQk3LEORH phc-

years to pass a judgement or may it be the attacks by the seculars residing not only in India but all around the world. Further in this chapter I will mention few heinous atrocities which Hindus had to face over so many decades, yet Hindus remain the most tolerant religion on the planet. It will not be possible for me to mention all because, for mentioning all the crimes against Hindus I will have to write another 50 more volumes. So for this reason I will mention a few crimes which can go down in history as the most terrifying crimes against any community.

1. The Mughal Era- Since in this chapter I will be talking about the major atrocities against Hindus, I will start the series of this brutality since the Mughal period which all the way continues yet now in this 21st century. 47,000 premiere temples were demolished during the Mughal period. *The genocide suffered by the Hindus of India at the hands of Arab, Turkish, Mughal and Afghan occupying forces for a period of 800 years is as yet formally unrecognised by the World.* With the invasion of India by Mahmud Ghazni about 1000 A.D., began the Muslim invasions into the Indian subcontinent and

Never forget the atrocities

they lasted for several centuries.[24] Nadir Shah made a mountain of the skulls of the Hindus he killed in Delhi alone. Babur raised towers of Hindu skulls at Khanua when he defeated Rana Sanga in 1527 and later, he repeated the same horrors after capturing the fort of Chanderi. Akbar ordered a general massacre of 30,000 Rajputs after he captured Chithorgarh in 1568. The Bahamani Sultans had an annual agenda of killing a minimum of 100,000 Hindus every year. The history of medieval India is full of such instances. The holocaust of the Hindus in India continued for 800 years, till the brutal regimes were effectively overpowered in a life and death struggle by the Sikhs in the Panjab[25] and the Hindu Maratha armies in other parts of India in the late 1700's. More than 6 million Hindus were killed in genocides by the Islamic rulers. When Mahmud of Ghazni entered Somnath on one of his annual raids, he slaughtered all 50,000 inhabitants. Aibak killed and enslaved hundreds of thousands. The list of horrors is long and painful. These

---

[24] https://www.sikhnet.com/news/islamic-india-biggest-holocaust-world-history
[25] https://www.sikhnet.com/news/islamic-india-biggest-holocaust-world-history

conquerors justified their deeds by claiming it was their religious duty to smite non-believers. Cloaking themselves in the banner of Islam, they claimed they were fighting for their faith when, in reality, they were indulging in straightforward slaughter and pillage. The Afghan ruler Mahmud al-Ghazni invaded India no less than seventeen times between 1001 – 1026 AD. The book 'Tarikh-i-Yamini' – written by his secretary documents several episodes of his bloody military campaigns : "The blood of the infidels flowed so copiously [at the Indian city of Thanesar] that the stream was discoloured, notwithstanding its purity, and people were unable to drink it…the infidels deserted the fort and tried to cross the foaming river…but many of them were slain, taken or drowned… Nearly fifty thousand men were killed."In the contemporary record – ' Taj-ul-Ma'asir' by Hassn Nizam-i-Naishapuri, it is stated that when Qutb-ul- Din Aibak (of Turko – Afghan origin and the First Sultan of Delhi 1194-1210 AD) conquered Meerat, he demolished all the Hindu temples of the city and erected mosques on their sites. In the city of Aligarh, he converted Hindu inhabitants to

Islam by the sword and beheaded all those who adhered to their own religion. The Mughal emperor Babur (who ruled India from 1526 - 1530 AD) writing in his memoirs called the 'Baburnama' – wrote : " In AH 934 (2538 C.E.) I attacked Chanderi and by the grace of Allah captured it in a few hours. We got the infidels slaughtered and the place which had been Daru'l-Harb (nation of non-muslims) for years was made into a Daru'l-Islam (a muslim nation)."In Babur's own words in a poem about killing Hindus (From the 'Baburnama') he wrote " For the sake of Islam I became a wanderer,I battled infidels and Hindus,I determined to become a martyr,[26] Thank God I became a Killer of Non-Muslims!". Banda Singh Bahadur was tortured to death after being imprisoned for 3 months. The heart of Banda Singh's son was put in his mouth in an attempt to humiliate him. Aurangzeb killed countless Hindus in his reign. He captured wife and 2 sons of Guru Gobind Singh. The wife was killed by freezing unto death and the 2 sons who aged 6 years and 8 years were asked

---

[26] https://www.sikhnet.com/news/islamic-india-biggest-holocaust-world-history

to convert. They clearly refused and finally accepted death over adharma and were brutally beheaded. He plundered the rich temples of Varanasi and build Gyanvapi Mosque on the Gyanvapi temple there. Finally, Akbar who is considered as 'AKBAR THE GREAT 'in our history textbooks and often referred to as so called secular labelled himself as 'Ghazi'. Ghazi means, the one who fights against non-Muslims. He killed 30,000 Rajputs and killed countless other Hindus. The most miserable thing was that this man collected the ' JANEU' which is a sacred thread which Hindus wear after killing them and weighed it to humiliate Hindus. It weighed 2980 kilos[27]. Yet he is referred as a great king. This is the tragedy. The question is Why we should remember and know all this? The biggest holocaust in World History has been whitewashed from history. When we hear the word HOLOCAUST most of us think immediately of the Jewish holocaust. Today, with increased awareness and countless cinema films and television documentaries – many of us are also aware of the Holocaust of the Native American peoples,

---

[27] https://youtu.be/OBCLD857xVo?feature=shared

the genocide of the Armenian peoples in the Ottoman Empire, and the millions of African lives lost during the Atlantic slave trade. Europe and America produced at least a few thousand films highlighting the human misery caused by Hitler and his army. The films expose the horrors of Nazi regime and reinforce the beliefs and attitude of the present-day generation towards the evils of the Nazi dictatorship. In contrast look at India. There is hardly any awareness among the Indians of today of what happened to their ancestors in the past, because a great majority of historians are reluctant to touch this sensitive subject. The Indian historian Professor K.S. Lal estimates that the Hindu population in India decreased by 80 million between 1000 AD and 1525 AD, an extermination unparalleled in World history. This slaughter of millions of people occurred over regular periods during many centuries of Arab, Afghan, Turkish and Mughal rule in India. Many Indian heroes emerged during these dark times – including the 10th Sikh Guru – Guru Gobind Singh and also the Hindu Maratha king – Shivaji Maratha – who led the resistance against this tyranny and eventually led to its defeat by the late 1700s — after centuries of death and destruction. The worst part is today we see in states like congress ruled Karnataka that Tipu Jayanti and Aurangzeb are celebrated openly.

2. The British Era- I have seen people appreciate British so much for the work they stupidly think they have done. Some of those are bringing trains to India and abolishing the tradition of Sati in Bharat and what not. Before I talk about the harm British have done towards Hindus, let me debunk this hoax of British abolishing sati theory. Sati was not a tradition of Hindus. There is not a single Hindu scripture which says that a woman should burn in the same fire as the husband, if the husband died before. There is no such reference for any such type of tradition. So the question is, how did the tradition of sati or Jauhar started in Bharat? The answer is, when the Islamic rulers tried to invade kingdoms ruled by Rajputs or any Hindu community, if they won that war, they captured the women of that kingdom and did all the brutal things you can imagine with them. The queens and all other women who belonged to that kingdom

thought it was better to burn in the fire instead of getting tortured by those heart-less and cruel Islamic rulers. This was the original reason because of which the concept of Sati or Jauhar was started. British had no contribution in abolishing the tradition of Sati. It was the Hindu society who finally decided that this tradition should not be continued any further. The history you were taught was WRONG. This is the real truth about the tradition of Sati which many of so-called educated people think was abolished by Britishers and is a part of Hinduism. Generally British Christians propagated that they built railways and roads in India and hence facilitated development. They actually built railways and roads for their convenience to loot India and not for the benefit of people of India. Many countries-built railways and roads without being colonised. Roads and railways were designed to carry raw materials from internal parts of India to the ports to be shipped to Britain. The first 2 chapters already give reference to the readers on how brutally and in a cruel way Britishers tried to wipe of Hinduism. And there are numerous Britishers and such incidences which will make you understand how cruel these Britishers actually were, but to understand the overall perspective, knowing how crooked Winston Churchill was is very important. The Nobel Prize-winning economist Amartya Sen has proved how in Bengal in 1943 Churchill engineered one of the worst famines in human history for profit. Over three million civilians starved to death whilst Churchill refused to send food aid to Bharat. Instead, Churchill trumpeted that "the famine was their own fault for breeding like rabbits." Churchill intentionally hoarded grain to sell for profit on the open market after the Second World War instead of diverting it to starving inhabitants of a nation controlled by Britain. Churchill's actions in Bharat unquestionably constituted a crime against humanity. Prior to Bharat's independence from Britain, Churchill was eager to see bloodshed erupt in Bharat, so as to prove that Britain was the benevolent "glue holding the nation together". For Churchill, bloodshed also had the added strategic advantage that it would also lead to the partition of Bharat and Pakistan. Churchill's hope was this partition would result in Pakistan remaining within Britain's sphere of influence. This, in turn, would enable the Great Game against the Soviet empire to continue, no matter the cost to innocent Bharatiyas and Pakistanis. The partition of Bharat with Pakistan caused the death of about 2.5 million people and displaced some 12.5 million others. In the beginning of this book, I have already mentioned how the Christian missionaries tried to eradicate Hinduism and impose Christianity on every single individual.

3. Khilafat Movement by Gandhi- Many of you must have read about the Khilafat movement in your school textbooks. The school textbooks as always teach you the wrong knowledge. The school textbooks do teach you that khilafat was an extremely successful movement started by Gandhi to unite Hindus and Muslims. But was it really so successful? Were the Hindus and sentiments of Hindus not harmed during this movement. Here is the truth about how this blunder of khilafat movement was hidden from you for so long. Muslims started this khilafat movement after World War 1 against British because the

caliphate of ottoman turkey was defeated. Gandhi assumed that this issue would be great point to unite Hindus and Muslims. But it turned out that this support from Gandhi towards Muslims resulted in mass murder of countless Hindus. So this movement was headed by Mohammed Ali and Shaukat Ali, popularly known as Ali brothers. Well, Mohammed Ali was no ordinary guy. He had studied in the Islamic system of education and also studied in oxford for his higher education. He was also some kind of bureaucrat in the Baroda government for some time and then later became one of the founding members of All India Muslim League, which we all know later became the main reason for partition. By the time these Ali brothers became the leaders of the Khilafat committee, their authority was nearly unchallenged. These two brothers toured all over India from 1919 to 1921 to gain support for the khilafat committee but got negligible support from people. But surprisingly, suddenly these 2 brothers got an unwavering support from the most unexpected quarters of masses in India. Which transformed this committee into a movement.

And this unconditional support came from Mohandas Karamchand Gandhi. So now because of Gandhi a huge mass of Hindus was supporting the khilafat movement now. This support for the khilafat movement resulted in mass murder of Hindus itself and the only person responsible for this blunder was Gandhi. Few of the conditions which Gandhi imposed on Hindus for this movement to be successful are as follows:

a. Hindus must not insist on prohibition of cow slaughter by Muslims at all.[28]

b. Hindus must abandon learning Hindi and start learning Hindustani, Urdu or Farsi.[29]

c. Hindus must not carry processions in front of mosques.[30]

d. Hindus must not play bhajans, kirtans etc if it offends Muslims.[31]

e. If Muslims attack Hindus unprovoked, Hindus must gladly submit to them by

---

[28] https://youtube.com/shorts/fG2sADIiAos?feature=shared
[29] https://youtube.com/shorts/fG2sADIiAos?feature=shared
[30] https://youtube.com/shorts/fG2sADIiAos?feature=shared
[31] https://youtube.com/shorts/fG2sADIiAos?feature=shared

brave appeals to the goodness of the hearts of Muslims and they must not retaliate.[32]

f. No matter how outrageous, no matter how extreme, Hindus had to meekly and blindly accept every single demand even if it meant death.

4. The Moplah Massacre- The support of the Indian leaders to the Khilafat movement (1919-1924) was a blow that India perhaps never recovered from. The Khilafat movement was one by Indian Muslims to support the Caliphate in Turkey. Essentially, the Indian leaders, especially Mohandas Karamchand Gandhi thought that by extending support to the Khilafat movement, he would get Indian Muslims to fight against the British and participate in the non-cooperation movement. He thought that Indian Muslims would join the nationalist movement in masses if he supported their demand for an Islamic caliphate.[33] What followed was mindless fanaticism by the Moplah Musalmans that resulted in the brutal murder of over 10,000

---

[32] https://youtube.com/shorts/fG2sADIiAos?feature=shared
[33] https://www.opindia.com/2021/09/what-mk-gandhi-said-moplah-genocide-of-hindus-1921-support-khilafat/

Hindus, the rape of thousands of Hindu women and the desecration of temples that Hindus held sacred. During the Malabar massacre in 1921, the Moplah Muslims went on a murder frenzy killing Hindus in the most brutal manner. On one particular incident on the 25th of September 1921, the Moplah Muslims massacred 38 Hindus by beheading them and throwing them in the well. It has been documented by the district collector of Malabar at the time how even after 2-3 days, several Hindus who were beheaded and thrown in the well were crying out for help. The Malabar massacre of 1921 was not the only time Moplah Muslims had unleashed genocide against Hindus. In the book written by the then Deputy Collector Diwan Bahadur C. Gopalan Nair, he has documented over 50 incidents of communal strife when the Muslims of Malabar had heaped atrocities against Hindus. Despite the history, the Indian leadership's response at the time was shameful, to say the least. Mohandas Karamchand Gandhi had extended unquestioning support to the Khilafat movement by the Malabar Muslims in the hopes that it would turn

Muslims into 'nationalists' resulting in them fighting the British empire in unison with Hindus. While the Malabar Muslims were slaughtering Hindus, raping women and forcefully converting Hindus, Mohandas Karamchand Gandhi insisted that they had committed a sin against the "Khilafat movement" and not the Hindus. In fact, he went ahead and insisted that Hindus must remain "non-violent" in the face go "extreme provocation". Further, Gandhi said that even if it were true that the Muslims were converting Hindus by force, the Hindus must not let this "put a strain on the Hindu-Moslem unity and break it". Of course, for Gandhi, the rapes, murders and forced conversions were not breaking the unity but Hindus, who were being persecuted, could potentially break that "unity" by getting mildly angry about their own persecution. [34]

5. Rangila Rasool Incident- Three books published in 1920 titled — ***"Krishna Teri Gita Jalani Padegi", "Unnisvi Sadi Ka Lumpat Maharishi"*** and ***"Sita Ka Chinaala"***

---

[34] https://www.opindia.com/2021/09/what-mk-gandhi-said-moplah-genocide-of-hindus-1921-support-khilafat/

by anonymous authors and publishers were published and freely distributed for 2–3 years through all Mosques in India. These books were disgustingly vulgar, containing obscene and appalling sketches of Hindu deities and sickening abuse and vile character assassination of Lord Krishna, Dayanand Saraswati and Ma Sita. When this matter reached Gandhi he justified it with the ***sickular*** logic of "Freedom of Speech". In 1923, after about three years, the Hindus tired of suppressing their anger and with no respite coming from any corner, published two books titled ***"Shaitan"*** referring to Mohammad being complete opposite of how a Prophet should be, and ***"Rangeela Rasool"*** (Colourful/Promiscuous Prophet) through Public Printing press in Lahore & Mahashay Rajpal's Lahore-based "Rajpal Publishers" respectively. The author was kept unknown and instead was described as one who will do ***"doodh ka doodh aur paani ka paani"*** The real author of that book was Pandit Chamupati (Krishan Prashaad Prataab), a well-known scholar of Koran and Islam. Rangeela Rasool revealed details which shouldn't had been revealed so publicly as it is in the Koran and had a surface appearance of a lyrical and laudatory work on him and his teachings; for example, it began with a poem which went "The bird serves the flowers in the garden; I'll serve my Rangila Rasul", and called it *"a widely experienced"* person who was best symbolized in a few inappropriate ways, in contrast with the lifelong celibacy of Hindu saints. Originally written in Urdu, it has been translated into Hindi. It remains banned in India, Pakistan and Bangladesh. Rangila Rasool sold all over India for a good one and a half years. But, suddenly in May, 1924, Gandhi with his sick policy of **extreme Muslim appeasement** decided to spring into action and threw out of the window his earlier justification of abuse of Hindu faith by invoking the right to **Freedom of Expression and Speech** as well as **Ahinsa.** He wrote a long article in his newspaper column ***"Young India"*** strongly condemning Rangeela Rasool saying " An ordinary and petty publisher in order to earn a few more bucks has insulted Prophet Mohammad and Muslims should punish those who write such books themselves!". Gandhi's these few lines implied tacit approval of *'Hinsa'* by Muslims towards Hindus. Yes, Gandhi was advising *'Hinsa'* with double standards — Muslims can be violent towards Hindus but the vice versa is not applicable. As Gandhi always vomited in all his speeches later too that Hindus should forever remain Ahinsawadi and cowards and not have the thought of even self-defence against Muslims!!! Khilafat movement's Maulana Mohammad Ali and one of Gandhi's favorite announced from Jama Masjid that **"Kaafir Rajpal should not be spared! He should be punished**". This article of Gandhi's and Mohammad Ali's Jama Masjid Islamic Jihad exhortment, gave Muslims all over India the opportunity and justification they were waiting for to kill Hindus in the name of religion. As a result, Mahashay Rajpal was attacked many times by Muslims and not surprisingly, not even a single verbal or written word from Gandhi throughout the years of the attacks on Mahashay Rajpal in his Muslim appeasement newspaper "Young India". Gandhi was fine with this *'Hinsa'* towards Hindus by Muslims as he had already given his tacit approval to it in his earlier article in "Young India". Muslim scholars filed a case on the book "Rangeela Rasool" in the lower Courts of Lahore in 1924, where Mahashay Rajpal was held guilty of Section 153A IPC and he appealed against it in the Lahore High Court. Gandhi then again wrote another provocative article hinting at this in "Young India" on 3rd Aug 1924 that "When a person does not get justice from Courts, he should try himself to become the judge." He was indirectly exhorting Muslims to take Law into their own hands. Then in 1927, under pressure from the Muslim community, the administration of the British enacted Hate Speech Law Section 295A as a part of the Criminal Law Amendment Act XXV. This made it a criminal offense to insult the founders or leaders of any religious community and is a version of anti-Blasphemy Law. This is the origin of Muslim appeasing hate speech Law 295A. In 1929, when the Lahore High Court Judge asked the Islamic scholars who were the petitioners to cite any false line or information in the book. The four Islamic scholars had no answer and agreed that it was a true historical narration of Mohammad and thus Mahashay

Rajpal was acquitted after a five-year court case. The fifth attack on Mahashay Rajpal by a Muslim carpenter named Mohammad Ilm Din proved fatal and took his life. He was stabbed multiple times on his chest and neck. Gandhi was in Lahore for around 7 days post this murder but he never went to Mahashay Rajpal's family to console his death. Neither did he ever write anything about this. The whole Hindu community thus stood up and took the matter to Court to sentence Mohammad Ilm Din for this murder through the Legal Justice system. And here again, Gandhi jumped in blindly defending Muslims and personally wrote a letter to the British Viceroy requesting him to forgive Mohammad Ilm Din and avoid giving him the death sentence. He also wrote one more article in "Young India" at that time stating that Mohammad Ilm Din was an innocent, young, immature, poor carpenter who was religiously incensed by the book Rangeela Rasool and thus subconsciously resulted in him committing the act of murder. Also Barrister Mohammad Ali Jinnah on request of poet Allama Iqbal, of "Saare Jahan Se Achcha" fame and is Pakistan's spiritual founder and National Poet, appeared as a defence lawyer of Mohammad Ilm Din in the Lahore High Court with the same argument as Gandhi's and requested the court to give him life imprisonment instead of the gallows and send him off Ilm Din to Kaala paani jail. The British however feeling threatened by the Hindu fury, executed Mohammad Ilm Din in Lahore Jail on 31st October 1929. Two days later Gandhi wrote in "Young India" that it was a 'black day' of history. Mohammad Ilm Din was immediately given the title "Hazrat Ghazi" (Honourable Slayer of Infidels/Protector of Islam) and "Shaheed (Islamic Martyr) " by Muslims and around 600,000 people attended his funeral. Many Islamic leaders like Mohammad Ali Jinnah and Allama Iqbal also attended his funeral where Iqbal was infact one of the carriers of the funeral bier. At that moment, Iqbal said, "Asi wekhde reh gaye, aye Tarkhaana da munda baazi le gaya" (The educated people like us just could do nothing, while this carpenter"s son scored a point). Unsurprisingly, Ilm-ud-Din has been glorified in Pakistan as a great Islamic hero, a holy warrior, a ghazi, a shaheed, etc. A film was made in 1978 lionizing him and villainizing Mhashay Rajpal. There is a mosque commemorating his "great deed", In February 2013, the Chief Justice of the Lahore High Court heard arguments on the maintainability of a petition seeking the reopening of an 84-year-old Ilm-ud-Din case. In October of the same year in 2013, at the two-day celebrations for the 84th annual Urs of this "Ghazi Ilm Din Shaheed" in the Miani Sahib graveyard, thousands of devotees paid homage to him. This is the real ugly face of Pakistan which is nothing but hatred towards Kaafirs and love for Islamic Jihadis. While followers of Jihadi Islam are clear about their ideology and goals, the confused, deracinated and ahimsavadi secular Hindus like Gandhi try to make sense and infact obfuscate gross bigotry and hatred filled in the minds of Jihadi Muslims as freedom of Expression and Right to Religious belief even though the right extends to take other people's (read 'Kaafir') lives![35]

35

https://r.search.yahoo.com/_ylt=Awr.xFrZVUllR_AzPqFXNyoA;_ylu=Y29sbwNncTEEcG9zAzQEdnRpZAMEc2VjA3Ny/R

6. The Exodus Of Kashmiri Pandits- 700,000 Kashmiri pandits were forcefully driven out of the Kashmir. They were driven out from their own land. What is this country where the inhabitants of their own country are forced to become refugees in their own country. What type of country this is where Kashmir can settle 5700 rohingya Muslims but not Kashmiri Hindus who were original inhabitants of that land. The atrocities which happened in Kashmir during that dark period are such that I cannot even describe the acts of barbarity against the Kashmiri pandits. The Kashmir files, a recent film by Vivek Agnihotri depicting the massacre which happened with Kashmiri Hindus was opposed shamelessly by all those politicians and intellectuals who saw this heinous crime happening in front of their eyes. They even tried to call for a ban on that film. What is even happening in this country where the liberal groups and secular groups just keep their mouth shut on the genocidal

---

V=2/RE=1699333722/RO=10/RU=https%3a%2f%2fwww.opi
ndia.com%2f2021%2f04%2fthe-assassination-of-mahashay-
rajpal-the-publisher-of-rangeela-rasool-how-secularism-and-
freedom-of-expression-died-along-with-
him%2f/RK=2/RS=nR8G4tP42SgeQyet5cOo7wbXpXI-

killings happening on Hindus. Is the definition of being a secular or liberal for them become being anti-Hindu. If it is so then these leftist liberals or seculars, whatever you call them should be completely eradicated from the country. So many victims had to suffer because of this mass genocide. The biggest tragedy was our sitting prime minister Dr. Manmohan Singh awarded Yasin Malik. A terrorist responsible for killing 42 Kashmiri Hindus or probably even more. The worst part is the supreme court of India rejected re-opening of cases of atrocities against Kashmiri Hindus because too much time had elapsed. This is the bloody discrimination happening against Hindus in their own country. The worst problem is that the media in our country has become so leftist that they will not even take the efforts to broadcast the atrocities which happened against Kashmiri Pandits. The congress government talking about the Manipur riots, is always silent when it comes Kashmir. Not a single congress leader condemns the genocide which happened in Kashmir, rather they call Kashmir files a propaganda film.

7. Countless Sacrifices for Building Ram Mandir-

Mir Baqi, Mughal emperor Babur's commander in chief ordered to demolish the great Ram Temple of Ayodhya and build Babri Masjid over it[36]. This demolition took place in roughly about 1528. One of the most holy shrine or temple for Hindus was wickedly destroyed by Babur and his army. Since then it was a civilisational memory of the Hindus that the particular place where the Babri Masjid was built is actually the Ram Janmabhoomi temple. This civilisational memory was carried on by Hindus for centuries until on 6 December 1992 the thousands of *karsevaks* scaled the walls of the Babri structure brought it to ground. However, it took another 27 agonising years for Hindus to win the decades long dispute over the ownership of the disputed land in Ayodhya. In 2019, the Supreme Court of India put an end to the long legal struggle and awarded the land to the Hindus, paving the way for the construction of

---

[36]

https://r.search.yahoo.com/_ylt=AwrgzfqLVkllgmw0EjRXNyo A;_ylu=Y29sbwNncTEEcG9zAzIEdnRpZAMEc2VjA3Ny/RV =2/RE=1699333900/RO=10/RU=https%3a%2f%2fen.wikipedi a.org%2fwiki%2fDemolition_of_the_Babri_Masjid/RK=2/RS=1 4jXJ0MOF3Z.R_2eP8p5j_B62Rs-

a *bhavya*(magnificent) Ram Mandir in Ayodhya. In the own country of Hindus it took so long to build a temple for Hindus which they consider as one of the most sacred. 47,000 temples were demolished by the Islamic rulers, but Hindus did not even ask for all those temples back. It is only Mathura, Kashi and Ayodhya temples which the Hindus want back. Ram Mandir took almost 30 years to be rebuilt. God knows when the verdict of Mathura and Kashi will come in favour of Hindus. But the story does not end here. Some incidences which show how ill-treated Hindus were during 1990s. On 2 November 1990, orders from the powers that be to then IG SMP Sinha were clear. The Mulayam Singh government in Uttar Pradesh <u>reportedly</u> asked him to clear the streets occupied by *karsevaks* who were peacefully demonstrating to reclaim Ram Janmabhoomi. Sinha told his subordinates: There is a clear instruction from Lucknow that the crowd will not sit on the streets at any cost. It was 9 am on the auspicious day of Kartik Purnima when Hindu saints and thousands of *karsevaks*, comprising also of women and elderly people, resumed their march towards the Ram Janmabhoomi site where the disputed structure then stood. The security forces, who were instructed to stop the Hindus from reaching the site, lined up on the road to block the way. Whenever the security personnel tried to impede the Hindu devotees, they would sit there and start chanting the name of Lord Ram and reciting Bhajans (religious songs). They touched the feet of the security personnel, deployed to prevent them from marching ahead. Each time they did this the security personnel would move back and the *karsevaks* would move forward. Though unarmed, the *karsevaks* remained undeterred. This kept happening in a loop until the IG passed orders and the police personnel sprung to action. Tear gas shells were fired, lathis were rained at the *karsevaks*, but the resolute Ram Bhakts neither counter-attacked nor did they agitate or falter. Suddenly the security personnel started responding by opening fire. Many Hindu devotees were targeted and gunned down. It's believed that the security personnel hunted and targeted Hindus in every lane and bylane leading to the Ram Janmabhoomi and within no time the streets converted into a war zone. The security personnel neither offered help to the injured nor allowed anyone else to help them. The police did not have any prior written order for firing. In fact, the district magistrate had signed the order after the police had carried out the firing. No *karsevak* was shot in the leg. All of them were shot in the head and chest. Which means that the security personnel had fired with an intention to kill and not injure.

8. Godra Hatya Kand- 27 February 2002: Remember the date. It was the day 59 Hindus returning from Ayodhya after performing karseva (voluntary labour) for the bhavya Ram Mandir. A disputed structure often referred to as 'Babri Masjid' stood on the land where once a temple dedicated to Shri Ram was there. Shri Ram was born in Ayodhya and that was his janmabhoomi (birthplace). On 6 December 1992, the structure was demolished by Hindus. That led to largescale communal violence. As revenge, on 12 March 1993, serial bomb blasts took place in Mumbai. The Babri demolition has been a bone of contention and cause of communal discord for decades now. It is a no brainer, hence that when 59 people, including women and

children were burnt live on 27 February 2002 inside a train by a riotous Muslim mob, it was because they were returning from Ayodhya. A place where they wanted to build Ram Mandir. A place where 'Babri Masjid' stood. Those burnt alive were all Hindus. Justice Nanavati Committee report talks about how the Godhra carnage took place. Right after the Godhra platform and boundary, there is a road and a locality named 'Signal Falia'. "It extends upto the culvert and goes further towards A cabin. It is a locality mainly inhabited by Ghanchi Muslims," the report mentions. When the train had arrived, a lot of unauthorised vendors, mainly Ghanchi Muslims, would come on platform and sell snacks, cold drinks, bidis, etc. The report further states that the train arrived at the platform at 7:43 AM as it was running about 5 hours late and there was a halt of about 5 minutes. In its evidence portion, the report cites media reports from 28th February 2002, the day after carnage, where leading mainstream media had reported that a mob has set Hindus on fire. They mentioned how Hindus were returning from karseva and how the mob set the train coaches on fire with petrol. While the attack by the

Muslim mob where 59 Hindus were burnt alive became the subject of several conspiracy theories peddled by the likes of Mukul Sinha, simply to save the riotous mob, even 20 years on, there are details of the carnage that are less spoken about. For example, while activists, NGOs and "secular" politicians tried to whitewash the burning alive of 59 Hindus, the less talked about aspect of what happened in 2002 is the fact that there was a second attack on Sabarmati Express only a few hours after the Hindus were burnt alive – the Muslim mob had come back to inflict more damage than they already had[37]. **THERE WAS ALSO A SECOND ATTACK ON SABARMATI EXPRESS WHICH NOBODY TALKS ABOUT**[38]. After the first attack on the train that

---

[37]

https://r.search.yahoo.com/_ylt=AwrO687pVkllKmkytzxXNyo A;_ylu=Y29sbwNncTEEcG9zAzEEdnRpZAMEc2VjA3Ny/RV =2/RE=1699333993/RO=10/RU=https%3a%2f%2fwww.opind ia.com%2f2022%2f02%2fgodhra-carnage-islamist-mob-returned-kill-hindus-train%2f/RK=2/RS=10afTLfhheF4MUTKZEQS18z.GUA-

[38]

https://r.search.yahoo.com/_ylt=AwrO687pVkllKmkytzxXNyo A;_ylu=Y29sbwNncTEEcG9zAzEEdnRpZAMEc2VjA3Ny/RV =2/RE=1699333993/RO=10/RU=https%3a%2f%2fwww.opind ia.com%2f2022%2f02%2fgodhra-carnage-islamist-mob-returned-kill-hindus-train%2f/RK=2/RS=10afTLfhheF4MUTKZEQS18z.GUA-

took place at 7:43 AM, administration got into action to make sure law and order and peace is maintained. The Nanavati-Mehta Commission then talks about the second attack that took place on the Hindus in the train by a 2,000-2,500 strong Muslim mob. RPF Commandant Pandey had rushed to Godhra and he said that when he reached near the train he had heard announcements made from the nearby mosque through a loud speaker. They were: "Kafiro ko mar dalo, Islam Khatre me Hai." Soon, a mob of 1,000 people armed with swords and sticks arrived from Signal Falia side. He asked the mob to back off, but when they didn't relent, he ordered his RPF men to open fire. Vikramsinh had fired 16 rounds from his carbine. H.C. Jhala had fired two rounds. Sub-Inspector Mr. Varma had fired 1 round from his pistol. Some rounds were fired by other policemen too. DY SP Simpi too had seen the mob of 2,000-2,500 people ready to attack the train again near the Ali Masjid. "At that time he had also heard announcements like "Islam Khatreme Hai, Maro, Kapo" coming from loud speakers of the Ali Masjid. He has stated that he can give the names of the injured policemen after seeing the record," the committee report says. PI Mehbubbeg Mirza, then a PI at CID, Vadodara, left for Godhra at 9:30 AM. He reported to Dy S.P. Simpi at about 11:20 and he asked to make the passengers sit in the train. While he was doing so, a mob of about 2500 to 3000 persons had come from the Signal Falia side. Persons therein were shouting 'Chhod Do, Mar Dalo, Kat Dalo". They were also throwing stones, he said. "He has stated that the mob which was seen coming from the Signal Falia side was trying to come near the train. When it was warned it was about 50 to 100 feet away from the train," he had said. While PI Mirza had not heard the announcement from the mosque, he heard the people in the mob chanting similar slogans. Nanavati-Mehta Commission report thus states, "The Commission does not find any good reason for rejecting their evidence. It is of the view that the evidence given by these witnesses is quite reliable and deserves to be accepted. It clearly establishes that the attack by the mobs on the train between 11.00 a.m. and 11.45 a.m. did take place as stated by the witnesses. This incident though it had happened after burning of coach S/6 is relevant as it is connected with what happened earlier between 8.00 a.m. and 8.30 a.m." Also remember the same type of killings did happen after Mohandas Gandhi was killed. With a few hours of assassination of Gandhi by the legendary saviour Nathuram Godse the caste of the assassins was published across country and orders came from the very top that people will have to pay price for it. The same evening a pogrom against one community started where every single person may it be woman or a child were burnt alive if it was found that their surname is Godse. This barbaric way of killing did not stop here, later on this extended to all the Chitpawan brahmins, Deshasthas and all other Maharashtrian Brahmins. Entire villages and towns like Bombay, Pune, Nagpur, Satara, Sangli, The Patwardhan princely states, Miraj, Kolhapur and Belgaum which is in current day Karnataka were ethnically cleansed same as Kashmiri Pandits.[39]

I had to mention about all these barbaric genocides which has happened against Hindus since centuries and we have forgotten the real past. We all were forced to forget are true past.

---

[39] https://youtube.com/shorts/Zr4vgxdMaMc?feature=shared

The main reason to mention all these genocidal killings against Hindus was to make you understand that how brutally people from different religions specially Christianity and Islam have consistently tortured Hindus but Hindus being the most tolerant community have tolerated it for so long. There are so many such incidents where Hindus were brutally killed either by Islamic rulers or the Christian missionaries. Every single Hindu was forced to covert. The one who refused was either made a slave or killed. This is the torture and atrocities are ancestors have handled for almost 1000 long years. Whatever we are today, leaving peacefully without any Sharia Laws imposed on us is because our ancestors fought bravely against these heinous crimes. So many of them also died fighting this battle. So never ever forget the past atrocities which happened against the Hindus. Because when past is forgotten, it is repeated. And if such past is repeated in any case in today's day and age, then we will definitely reach a point of no return where it will be impossible for us to save ourselves, our community and our culture from those barbaric killers. **SO, HINDUS PLEASE WAKE UP!!!**

COUNTLESS HINDU LIVES LOST FOR BUILDING THE RAM TEMPLE.

Never forget the atrocities

THE GODRA HATYA KAND VICTIMS WHO WERE BRUTALLY BURNT ALIVE.

INHUMAN ATTROCITIES BY MUGHALS ON HINDUS.

We were never a defeated civilisation.

Now that you know the basic guideline of what the true history is, let me pass onto you some knowledge which you should know. Have you ever wondered that even after such atrocities, brutalities and frequent mass genocidal killings we still managed to be 1.2 billion. How was this even possible? Was this possible if we were actually defeated? The way school teaches you about the history, it is very much obvious that you may think that we are a defeated civilisation. But to make such completely wrong and baseless judgements is not right. You should know the right perspective of the history, that is when you will truly understand that we are the only civilisation who survived the oppressions by Islam and Christianity. Here is the answer for the very famous question which lies in the head of amongst the major part of population of this country which is "WHY ARE WE A DEFEATED CIVILISATION AND WHY WE WERE COLONISED SO EASILY".

Firstly, I would like to mention that this whole question is historically completely incorrect. It is factually completely incorrect. To assume that we are a constantly invaded and defeated civilisation does such grave factual injustice to the kind of resistance that we have put up, the kind of fight that we have given and the way we re-conquered several portions. I am sorry but this question is historically baseless and there is a very valid reason for this. Each time this discussion happens the trap that you walk into is by looking at Bharat's experience as an isolated experience as if we are the only country that has constantly faced invasions and we have had no response mechanisms. The problem with that assumption is twofold. First one, look at the number of pre-Christian and pre-Islamic civilisations which have vanished in front of your eyes and which have been pushed to extinction over several centuries. Lithuania is perhaps the youngest Christian

We were never a defeated civilisation.

country relatively. They became Christian some 300-400 years ago. Compare that with Bharat which has retained its non-Christian and non-Islamic character to a significant extent and we continue to believe that we are invaded, that we are defeated and that we are easily colonised. Do you really believe that the number that we have today in terms of population is because of any lack of effort or intent on the part of the Muslim invader or Christian colonizer. Is that your understanding of history, please look at the number of Hindu princely states that the great Sardar Vallabhai Patel had to weave together and put together to create Indian Union. Look at the number of Hindu princely states that ultimately British took the power from. So clearly at least from the 18th century or the battle of Panipat and even significantly after that is after 1761, Hindus had re-conquered so many areas. Compare that with Africa, compare that with Latin America, North America, Australia or the rest of the world for that matter or even for that matter Europe. EUROPE IS NOT A CHRISTIAN CIVILISATION. At the outset it has become a

Christian Civilisation. Therefore, the very first defeated civilisation and the very first conquered civilisation is the European civilisation, which has completely lost its pre-Christian origins and its pre-Christian faith systems. Please take a look at what's happening in Lithuania and Iceland and so many other countries where they are trying to revive the faith systems which existed prior to Christianity. They are struggling to do so. But we still remain as the 3rd largest religion in the world. Take a look at what has happened with the Jews, look at all these experiences and you still think, that you are a defeated civilisation. That's the problem with history textbooks today. It teaches you that you are a defeated society. After the first invasion or let's say first major incursion which is invasion of Sindh by the Arabs in 711 CE, it took them close to 300 years to cross the Sindh. The frequent invasions and the regularity of invasions started in late 10th century. After that as a civilisation obviously you will have to take sometime to respond but what do you make of Rajputs, what do you make of Marathas, what do you make of the Sikhs. Somehow, we do

We were never a defeated civilisation. selectively celebrate all of them and still continue to believe that we are defeated civilisation. Does nobody teach you how the Dutch Navy lost at the hands of Marthananda Verma, the king of Travancore in the 18th century. He was the first Asian ruler to comprehensively defeat a European navy. Don't we read any of this? This question is actually reflective of the abysmal and disappointing lack of knowledge as far as Bharat's history is concerned. When you look at Bharat in isolation, you will assume that this is some kind of walk-in or walk-over where everybody's had a walk in the park to simply enter this place. Don't you know about the ruthless resistance which was given even to the Alexander. He was given among the toughest resistances that was ever known by the Brahmins and the ladies of the particular region which you know as the 'Vahik Pradesh' today which is commonly known as 'Bactrian' region. Read all this history. You have inherited a history of valour and huge resistance, and a successful resistance. Entire Spain was under Islamic rule for close to 800 years after which they had to launch

'Reconquista'. From the Bharatiya experience Reconquista has been going on right from the beginning. Ask the Rajasthanis and they will tell you about Bapa Raval. He was the one who actually kicked these fellows all the way to Arabia. Maharana Bapa Rawal defeated Mohammad Bin Qasim, the first attacker of Islam on Bharat and chased Arabs all the way up to Iran. On his way back, he erected guard posts at every hundred Kilometres manned by Rajput chiefs. This is the reason why Hindus kept Arabs at the bay for 300 years even after Bapa Rawal's death. Please read the history before you jump to these conclusions. Whatever you are taught is rubbish. It is garbage. It is not even worth recycling. Read the works of R.C Majumdar, Jadunath Sarkar, Har Bilas Sarda, G.C Pande, read the works of contemporary scholars like Dr. Meenakshi Jain or Sita Ram Goel. We are not children of Gandhi and you are not certainly children of some peace-loving hippie. You have taken forward and inherited a huge tradition of 'Kshatra', regardless of what you think of your 'Varna'. So please, negate this nonsense from your head and remove this rubbish from your head. If you have such questions then you know nothing about your history. The white-man wants us to think that we are a defeated society that's why your textbooks were designed in such a way. He wants us to think that we are a defeated society. What defeated society? Europe today is in shambles. It has no response to the challenge of the middle-east. Bharat has been dealing with this for several centuries and it has managed to contain what Europe is unable to contain. Sweden is effectively crumbling as a society as a result of illegal migrations. Germany doesn't want to talk about the mass rapes that happen in that particular country as a consequence of illegal migrations. Paris does not want to talk about certain suburbs which are no-go zones for the police anymore. That's exactly what is happening in the so-called west. They don't know how to handle this creature. We know how to handle this creature because we have been doing this for generations now. Please delete all the rubbish knowledge which you have in your head and start reading proper books if you truly want to question Bharat's history. I hope you do so and never ask such nonsensical questions ever again and you stop someone from asking this question again and shame him or her for asking such rubbish questions. This question is not a personal problem rather this question is a problem which us collective. Stop reading the Marxist school of nonsense. Their entire goal has been to push you into slavery. Don't at all read the literature by Romila Thapar, Irfan Habib or R.S Sharma. They are not worth reading at all under any circumstances. The only reason you should read them is to understand how paid stooges have effectively brushed Bharat's history under the carpet to the detriment of the civilisation. These people did not even have the guts or the courage or the conviction to actually prove their point in the Ram Janmabhoomi case. When they were invited to actually prove themselves and present themselves as expert witnesses, they kept peddling nonsense and propaganda as opposed to putting forth facts. So please don't read these books, they are not worth reading at all. There is no such history as the history of north and the south, Bharat has always been one. Are you telling me that after colonizing and

We were never a defeated civilisation.

converting several continents, the only reason you are alive today as Hindus is because of the benevolence of the Christian colonizer or invader, how is it even possible. Why will they even spare you if he did not spare whole of the world. This is because you fought back against them spiritually, politically, culturally, militarily and intellectually. Introspect why people even ask such questions. Is it coming from the position of knowledge or the darkness of ignorance. Who are people to even say we are a defeated civilisation. In fact, our ancestors have given the toughest fight and resistance to such invaders more than any other country. Zoroastrians were wiped off from the Iranian and Mesopotamian region with 15 years by Islam. it did not even take Islamic religions 60 years to wipe off almost all Abrahamic religions completely. But here, our ancestors have defended and protected not only us but even our culture.

At least respected those great individuals who sacrificed their lives just so that we can practice our culture freely. Stop being this liberal and secular hoax and accept the fact that to be secure in Bharat, a Hindu dominant country is needed. And to be safe a Hindu dominant country is not only important for Hindus but equally important to Muslims as well. Or else it is the history of this world that whenever a country has become a Muslim dominant country, democracy has died and most of the times Sharia Law has taken birth in its wildest forms. So, this is our duty as Hindus, we need to worship our ancestors and remember them so that we give them due respect the deserve. Countless people have sacrificed lives in the hope of saving Sanatan Dharma and helping it live by its meaning which is 'eternal'.

This is my humble request to everyone, please ensure that you try to preach people including your friends and families about the true history of our Bharat as much as possible and help them understand our true history which they never understood due to brainwashing. In this generation of internet, it has become so easy to access information. Try to research about the rich culture and past and tell people about it. Talking about it and preaching the right knowledge to people is truly going to help us a lot. I have seen people usually give excuse that they don't have enough time to preach people about all this. That is totally fine, just make sure that the way you have a corner of heart reserved from your family where there is enormous amount of love for them, same way just build a corner in your heart where you have unconditional love for your country and history. And this will truly help in bringing a real change in everyone's way of thinking.

Please read scriptures.

यः सर्वत्रानभिस्नेहस्तत्तत्प्राप्य शुभाशुभम् |
नाभिनन्दति न द्वेष्टि तस्य प्रज्ञा प्रतिष्ठिता || 57||

yaḥ sarvatrānabhisnehas tat tat prāpya śhubhāśhubham
nābhinandati na dveṣhṭi tasya prajñā pratiṣhṭhitā

Meaning- One who remains unattached under all conditions, and is neither delighted by good fortune nor dejected by tribulation, he is a sage with perfect knowledge.[40]

This is the last chapter of my book and the last milestone you need to accomplish to fully reawaken as a Hindu. This is not even a mere request from my side to you, rather I beg each and every one of you to read the Hindu

---
[40] https://www.holy-bhagavad-gita.org/chapter/2/verse/57

scriptures, especially the 'Bhagavad Gita'. I beg you to read it. This is not even an exaggeration but I would recommend my worst of the enemy to read the 'Bhagavad Gita'. As for Islam 'The Quran' is the holy book and as for Christians 'The Bible' is the holy book, same way 'Bhagavad Gita' is NOT the holy book of Hindus. It is more than that. The Gita is a life guide for every single individual on this planet. It is the most impactful book you will ever read. The Gita teaches you to be happy always. It helps you find the true meaning and purpose of life. It has so much meaning in itself that it is not even possible for me to describe the rich meaning of that book. It does not matter if you are atheist, or if you are a believer. Gita is a book meant for everyone to read. The most important thing which people should know is that the book is not meant to read by people after retirement or after the get old. Gita should be taught to children in a proper way. Reading Gita gives people true peace. This book 'REBUILDING SANATAN- A ROADMAP TO REAWAKEN HINDUS' would not have been possible if I wouldn't had read that book. I want each and every one of you who reads this book to reawaken yourself completely by reading the Gita. And please make sure you do not give the excuse of you don't have time to read the Gita. It is not about it anymore. It is a very important book which every single one of you should read.

Mark my words, it has got solution for every single problem in your life. If you are a non-Hindu reading this book, I even recommend you to read Gita. I promise you; you will never regret it. Once you read Gita completely with full devotion and seriousness, you will embark on a journey. Embark on a journey of not only reawakening yourself but also finding the true meaning and purpose of your life. Once you read the Gita you can go forward with finding a spiritual master for yourself or reading many other Hindu books such as Vedas, but that is a whole together a different journey. I want you to just get started with reading Bhagavad Gita. This will be one of the best decisions you will take in life.

I would like to conclude this chapter with a short story about Gita which I heard recently, so one book distributor went to a group of people in Russia and they were all drinking.

Please read scriptures.

And as soon as he went in and showed the books, everyone said get lost. But one of them said "stop, which books you have?" and he showed a whole list of books. This guy who said stop picked out Bhagavad Gita. In other hand was bottle of liquor and this one Bhagavad Gita he showed to his friends and said, "my dear friends, this Gita is very special". And the friends were drunk, they were bewildered thinking what has happened to this guy, is he drunk more and asking each other why is he speaking like this. He said, "actually I was going through a lot of depression and I was trying to find a solution and found this book, I tried to read the book but it was very hard. I couldn't understand anything and I gave up, but then after a few months I decided to give it a one more try. So, in vacation specifically I took this book and for whole month when I tried to understand it peacefully, every single word was like nectar." And finally, he realised that Gita is very special. So, although he was in high state, he could not change his habit fully but he developed appreciation for Gita because you really understand how your life can transform and change.

With this I would conclude this chapter lastly requesting you once again to start reading the Gita. It has solution for every single question of your life.

Epilogue

In a land where temples once did gleam
Now shrouded in a sorrow-laden dream
A civilization's ancient, sacred theme
Engulfed in the darkest, tumultuous stream
The rivers that flowed with tales of old
Bear witness to stories untold, unrolled
The tragedies and sorrows of stories they're told
As history weaves through the chapters of gold
In a realm where history's pages are stained
By the weight of countless sorrows, unchained
A civilization's past, forever pained
By brutalities and atrocities, ingrained
On the banks of sacred rivers, they weep
Where stories of faith and despair intertwine deep

Innocence shattered, their memories to keep
In a civilization's heart, the scars run steep
For eight long centuries, a solemn tale,
Hindus faced brutalities, their courage frail.
Through invasions and strife, they stood strong,
Their history marked by suffering and wrong.
Temples desecrated, culture under attack,
Yet they endured, striving to take their lives back.
In the face of darkness, they kindled a light,
Preserving their faith, their heritage, their might.
From ancient times to the present day,
Their resilience shines, a powerful display.
In unity and hope, they find their way,
Over eight centuries, a testament they convey.

So thereby, this is a basic roadmap which I was able to design at my individual capacity to encourage people to reawaken themselves. Last thing which I want to say before I conclude is that always remember HINDUS DO NOT HAVE THE LUXURY OF LOSING HOPE. We have to strive and work

Please read scriptures.

hard to continue our legacy which our great ancestors have passed on. Hindus are always forced to reform themselves by every single government. Even the supreme court of India always tries to reform the Hindus. From restricting height ban on Dahi Handi to banning exhibiting snakes on Nag Panchami. From prohibiting Kulu Dusshera festival to overturning centuries old Sabarimala Tradition and so much more. Hindus have been constantly discriminated against. But we as Hindus have never become hopeless and we continue to pass our reach legacies forward. Finally, I am proud of every single Hindu out there who has constantly been discriminated against since decades even in independent India. Because even after such discrimination we has Hindus have adjusted with all kinds of governments and people. I am proud of all of you Hindus who are thriving to reawaken Hinduism.

www.ingramcontent.com/pod-product-compliance
Lightning Source LLC
LaVergne TN
LVHW061616070526
838199LV00078B/7306